ANECDOTES

FROM

MY LIFE

BY

DAVID HUDSON

TABLE OF CONTENTS

APOLOGIA PRO ANECDOTIA SUA

I have always been fascinated with the word "apologia". It makes what you say next sound like an apology, but it is not. It is a simple explanation of what is to follow. When Cardinal John Henry Newman wrote his "Apologia Pro Vita Sua", he was not apologizing for converting from Anglicanism to Roman Catholicism, but merely explaining the reasons, which were to him compelling. The following is simply an explanation, not an apology.

I am making no apologies for what I have written. On the contrary, I have found in the telling of these stories a pleasure and satisfaction which has been somewhat surprising to me. The pleasure is threefold. First is the pleasure of recalling events which, in many cases, I have not thought about for many years. Second has been the pleasure of an author who enjoys trying to find just the right words to tell his story. And third has been the pleasure in knowing (or assuming) that some part of me will not soon be forgotten by my descendants. Yes, I am that conceited!

I have been writing these anecdotes from time to time for the past two years or more. I hope to continue writing them as long as memory provides occasions to do so. They are not intended as autobiography, nor even as a memoir. Both types of writing require more continuity than I am attempting in this writing. I am simply remembering for myself some of the funny or beautiful or sad or troubled times that have happened to me during a surprisingly extended lifetime of more than eighty years. As long as this amuses me, I hope to continue writing and sharing the results.

I should caution you, also that, memory being what it is, I make no guarantee that these events happened exactly as I describe them. This is how I remember them, which is not necessarily the same thing at all.

I hope that no one will take offense at what I write. Everyone I write about I remember with affection,[1] and gratitude that you have shared your life with me. I keep discovering over and over that life is a lot of fun, especially if you let others share it with you. I didn't know that sixty years ago, but I have learned it over time. I'm a slow learner, but not hopelessly dense. If I have a philosophy of life, that is it. Share your life as fully as possible with others.

David Hudson

---

[1] With the exception of Mrs. Smith—see **IV. Neighbors**

II

HOW WILLIE THE WHALE CHANGED MY LIFE

From a young age, music, in particular what we usually call "classical" music, has been very important in my life. The only one in my family who really cared about classical music was my father, who, although he played no instrument, loved to sing. However, the chances for him to indulge this love in small-town Iowa in the 1940s were few and far between. Sunday mornings were devoted to "sacred" music, hymns, and what I can only describe as "mediocre" choir anthems (i.e. anthems simple enough for even a totally untrained choir to sing). How, then, did I ever acquire a taste for great classical music?

The earliest classical music that I can recall hearing was when I was four years old and began attending pre-school, which was directed and taught by a young man named Lowell Colston, a member of Dad's church. This was during World War II, and Mr. Colston should have been in the army, except for one thing—he was so badly crippled, I presume by arthritis, that he could barely walk, even with the aid of a pair of crutches. His body may have been crippled, but his heart was not. He loved children, and reveled in the chance to teach us. He also loved good music, and not a day in pre-school went by without his playing something for us. Much of what I remember him playing was folk music, often classical arrangements of folk melodies. I remember one piece which was everyone's favorite, *Symphony on a French Mountain Air,* by Vincent D'Ande. It got played so often that

3

eventually a chip appeared on the edge of the disc, probably caused by one of us mishandling it. It made no difference. We endured the loss of the first 15 or 20 seconds, and still relished it. That was my first real exposure to "classical" music, and it took permanent hold on me.

Then when I was about five or six years old, I had a very serious illness, and was confined to bed for a week or better. At the best of times, I was never a very good patient, but as I began to feel better, I became a real problem for my mother to care for. I was demanding, whiny, and unreasonable about the need to stay in bed. My 16-year-old brother, Lewis, taking pity on her, decided to try to find a way to entertain me and give her a bit of a break from my incessant complaining. Taking his paycheck which he had just received from his recently acquired job (his first) he bought the album **"The Whale Who Wanted to Sing at the Met"**, for me to listen to and to give my mother a few minutes of peace. Why he chose this particular album, I have no idea, except that it was intended for children. At any rate, he presented it to me and moved the record player into my room.

I was enthralled. I loved the picture of a singing whale on the cover, and when I started to listen, it was a revelation to me. Hearing Willie the Whale sing Mephisto's majestic bass aria from Gounod's **Faust**, and even more, Figaro's introduction of himself from The **Barber of Seville**, was like nothing I had ever heard before.

But then, the terrible thing happened. Tetti-Tatti the opera impresario, thinking he was rescuing an opera singer from the belly of a whale, **harpooned** Willie! His friend Whitey the seagull cried. I

Cried!! I had never suspected that the world could be so cruel! But then the voice-over announcer (I never stopped to wonder where he came from) assured Whitey (and me) that Willie was now in heaven where he could sing in a hundred voices, each one more glorious than before. We then heard Willie (x 100) singing the grand chorus from the obscure opera **Martha**. In the seventy or so years since, I have never seen, or even heard, this entire opera, but that glorious chorus will always have a special place in my heart, because Willie sang it! By the time I was well and out of bed, I was hooked. Classical music of all varieties has ever since been one of my passions. And sometimes, when in a relaxed mood, I can still hear Willie singing "Figaro, Figaro, Figaro"!

As an adult, I have learned to appreciate many forms and types of music, even the popular music my sister loved, and I had scorned. But classical music became and has remained, my music of choice, and the one which usually carries the most meaning, comfort, and pleasure for me.

III

WHY I AM NOT A MAGICIAN

When I was about eight, our school presented a special treat for us. They invited a magician to do a show for the entire school. It was a special treat, and I for one, was enchanted. The magician could make things appear out of thin air, find silver dollars in students' ears, and make things disappear without apparently touching them. He could do things that I didn't even know were possible. I knew right then that I wanted to become a magician.

It was not long after that father found me tinkling around on our old piano, an activity that I engaged in from time to time when I was bored. He asked me whether I would like to learn to play the piano. Now you didn't just say flatly, "no" to my father. Not that he would punish me, but I knew he would be disappointed, and I didn't want that. So I used a child's time-honored ploy to get out of something I didn't really want to do. "Um, I don't know," (in my most disinterested voice). My father was no dummy and he knew I was saying no. "That's too bad," he said. "If you learned to play the piano, you might learn to become a musician." Oh, I thought, so that's how it's done! My attitude changed instantly. "I guess I would like to learn." My parents signed me up for lessons, and suddenly I was a piano student, but a very puzzled one almost from the start, because I didn't understand how this would help me become a magician. But since my father had said so, it must be true.

Thus began six months of pain for everyone involved, my parents (particularly my mother, who tried to enforce my practice), my teacher, and most of all me. I hated the piano! All this effort and all I could play were the simplest of melodies, which even to me were boring. Practice was torture. Piano lessons were occasions for fear because I knew I had not learned what I was assigned the previous week. The climax came six months later when my teacher had a recital for all her students. She had assigned to me the simplest of melodies which she thought I could learn. Of course, I didn't. Came the day of the recital, and terror set in. I knew I couldn't play, but now I had to reveal this in front of all these adults, many of whom were known to me because they were members of my father's church. I had no choice, I **refused** to play! It was either suffer the ire of my parents and my teacher, or forever humiliate myself in public. No coaxing could get me to the piano. The world never did get to hear "Twinkle, Twinkle" or whatever it was.

But I had made my point. No matter how much I wanted to be a magician, I was not going to go through this agony. My parents and my teacher consulted, and concluded that perhaps it would be wise to discontinue lessons, to my great relief. It must have been years later that I discovered that the two words were not the same. By then the desire to become a magician, let alone a musician, had long departed. Or as my oldest daughter Jennifer put it when she was about eighteen, when asked if she was a musician. "Momma and Laura and Beth are musicians. Daddy and I are appreciators."

IV

NEIGHBORS

I was born in Ottumwa, Iowa—or was it Bloomfield, Iowa? This was a true dilemma for me when I was young. I knew that I had been born in St. Joseph's Hospital in Ottumwa, but my parents at that time lived in Bloomfield. When confronted with forms to fill out when I was of grade school age, I was of two minds when asked for my birthplace. Shouldn't my birthplace be where I first lived? But that was not quite true. I had been born in a hospital in a neighboring town. The upshot was that I sometimes said "Ottumwa" and sometimes "Bloomfield", thereby creating that nightmare scenario for future genealogists—two or more primary records giving conflicting evidence. Ah, well—

My father was minister of the Bloomfield Christian Church, and we lived there until I was eight. My earliest memories are of there. One of them involves an old cistern in our back yard. It had a cement cover with a hole in the middle, perhaps three inches in diameter— perfectly safe for a child to play around. I remember how much fun it was to drop my toys through the hole to hear the satisfying *plunk*— and then crying because I wanted them back.

We lived on an unpaved street where there was little traffic. My older brothers and their friends played ball in the street because that was the largest nearby unencumbered area for games like football and baseball. One of their number was always designated as lookout, and on the few occasions when a car did appear, he would call out, "Car!"

and their game would be instantly suspended while they cleared the street. After the car passed, they would resume their game exactly where they had left off. I don't think my parents ever quite approved of this behavior, but they never actually forbid it. However, when I was playing in the yard, I was strictly forbidden ever to set foot in the street.

Which brings me (by a rather roundabout way) to the subject of this anecdote. On both sides of the parsonage lived elderly widows. I do not remember the name of the widow on the north side, so I shall just call her Mrs. Smith. On the south side lived Mrs. Bellis. Mrs. Bellis was a kindly lady who welcomed me and my younger brother to play around her house (being cautioned, however, not to damage her flowerbeds). Mrs. Smith, on the other hand, did not appear to have any use for small boys, and we were warned never to set foot on her property.

Mrs. Smith drove a Model A Ford, which even in those days was something of an antique. "Drive" is perhaps the wrong verb to use about what she did when she got behind the wheel—"aimed" might better describe it. When she backed her car out of her garage, it could end up anywhere. Often as not, it went right across our front yard. Our dining room had a large window which looked out on a rather small side yard, and onto Mrs. Smith's garage. One time while we were gathered as a family for the noon meal (we actually did that in those days!), we heard a large crash. We looked up just in time to see the back of her garage majestically swing upward, pause for a few seconds, and then, just as majestically, swing back down. Mrs. Smith apparently had put the car in a forward gear, rather than in reverse.

So, you can see that my parents were somewhat nervous about my playing in the front yard. I was cautioned that, whenever I saw Mrs. Smith heading for her garage or heard her car start up, I was to get up on the front porch immediately. Mrs. Smith was the subject of enough conversation in our family that I was somewhat afraid of her, so I was diligent in obeying my mother in this respect. (Any of you who conclude from this that I was a generally obedient child can forget about it. I could, however, be scared into obeying.)[2]

From this admonition and from watching my brothers play in the street, I developed a game. As I mentioned, cars were infrequent on our street, but there was some traffic. Whenever I saw any car coming, I would race up on the porch and hide. If I got safely on the porch before the car passed, I won. If not, I lost. By doing this I learned one of the principles which the famous psychologist, William James, had enunciated many years before. I never heard of William James or his work until I read him in college, but when he was talking about bravery (or some such thing), he declared that, "We do not run because we are afraid, but we are afraid because we run." By age four, I could vouch for that. I found that what started out as a game where I knew I was in no danger (except from Mrs. Smith, of course) began to feel very real. By the time I was on the porch, I was really afraid, despite knowing I was in no danger. I don't know how long I actually

---

[2] Since writing this, I have discovered an account written by my brother Lew about our next-door neighbor. Since he is ten years older than me, I must bow to his superior knowledge. The neighbor's name was Clara Rominger, and she was an unmarried, retired schoolteacher, whom it seems retired none too soon, and with a sour attitude about all children.

played this game (probably not very long), but its memory is still vivid, and one of the major memories of my early childhood.

Mrs. Bellis, on the other hand, was quite the opposite. She was kindly and loved little boys. Bill and I were almost always welcome to come visit her. In summer she often sat on her front porch in a swing, and we were welcome to come over and sit with her. She had a rock garden by the porch, which included a large conch shell. Whenever we came over, we would want to "listen to the sea" in it. She also had a yucca plant growing in that rock garden, the only one I had ever seen, since the plant is not native to Iowa. Its spiky leaves fascinated me. On the occasions when we were invited in for cookies, I particularly remember being charmed by her snow globe, the first one I had ever seen. In short, Mrs. Bellis was just the opposite in every way from Mrs. Smith.

However, Mrs. Bellis had one characteristic which didn't bother Bill and me, but was disturbing to many adults. She liked to make up stories—not stories to tell to children, but stories calculated to disturb her neighbors, and sometimes the whole community. Bloomfield had no black residents—whether by ordinance or tradition I do not know, but being only ten miles or so from the Missouri border, it had many of the characteristics of a southern town. So when Mrs. Bellis announced that she had sold her house to "six black boys," it created something of an uproar in the community. My father was amused by all this. For one thing his record as a progressive minister on racial issues in Texas meant that he wouldn't be upset. And secondly, he knew she didn't mean it. How this all was resolved, I don't know, but things were soon back to normal, and I suspect Mrs. Bellis had a good laugh over the way she had turned the community on its ear.

But hearing this all discussed in my family secured in my mind the idea that she wasn't always truthful in all things. One day in the spring of 1945 when the parsonage was being painted, Mrs. Bellis came out of her house, and seeing the painter up on his ladder slathering away with his brush, she called up to him "President Roosevelt just died." I don't know what the painter replied, but he never missed a stroke of his brush. I was playing in the yard and heard this. I was horrified. This was the worst lie I had ever heard! I didn't say anything until Mrs. Bellis went back into her house, but I had to do something to squelch this tale before it spread, so I called up to the painter and said, "You don't have to believe her, mister. She tells lies."

Alas for my brief career as a truth squad member. It was true.

No matter what her reputation in the truth-telling department, I remember Mrs. Bellis with great fondness as one of the positive influences on my childhood. Not so Mrs. Smith. To this day I remember her as a witch!

V

CALIFORNIA, HERE I COME!

I believe it was in 1948 when I took the first seriously long journey of my life. My father was the minister of the First Christian Church in Boone, Iowa. A part of his agreement with the church was that he would attend the International Convention of the Christian Churches each year at the church's expense. This convention was held once a year at a different city from coast to coast. The convention might be as close as Chicago or Indianapolis, or even Des Moines, or as far away as either coast.[3] In 1948 it was being held in San Francisco. My parents decided that this would make an excellent vacation for the entire family. You can imagine my joy when I heard that! I had never even been out of Iowa (little journeys to relatives in northern Missouri when we lived in Bloomfield didn't count).

There were, however, some difficulties. First of all the church would pay my father's expenses, but not that of the family. Some means would have to be made to minimize the expenses. Second, the convention took place in October, during the school year. That turned out not to be much of a problem. One word from my father, and our teachers quickly gave their assent. As one of them said, "Such a trip will be far more educational than three weeks in school." I was, I believe, in sixth grade and Bill was in third grade. Beth was in high school. She was far less enthusiastic than Bill and I were about this

---

[3]The "International Convention" is now called the "General Assembly" and is now held only every other year.

13

trip. In fact she was downright opposed to it. She was far more socially involved with her peers than I was, and did not relish the prospect of missing three weeks of this sort of interaction. She may also have had some sense of how much stress a cross-country trip confined in a car with her younger brothers might be. At any rate, she begged off. Mom and Dad agreed that she could stay with another family during this time, if she really did not want to go. However, two of my older brothers were anxious to go. The oldest, Dick, was a minister of a Christian Church in Chicago. He probably had a similar arrangement with his church concerning attendance, and hence was expected to go. My next oldest brother, Bob, was a religion student at Drake University at that time, and I believe was a student minister of the Christian Church in Stanhope, Iowa. Obviously, a small church such as that would not have had the same expectations or the resources, but Bob did not want to miss the opportunity to go with us. The six of us made a carload in that none-too-big Plymouth that my father drove.

My father made careful plans for this trip. Somewhere he bought a used tent-top camping trailer. None of us had ever seen anything like it before, and judging by the interest it aroused wherever we stopped, neither had most people. Camping trailers were known, of course, but not collapsible ones with a tent top. When closed, the trailer was quite compact, and quite efficiently aerodynamic. When we stopped for the night, two people could quite easily erect the tent-top in 10 minutes or less. It was quite efficiently designed, and six could sleep in it, if you were very good friends, or at least family.

Under normal circumstances my father would have considered this an unnecessary extravagance, but when he calculated the cost of three weeks of motel and hotel rooms for six people, the price probably looked very reasonable.

As with most long anticipated trips, at the last minute nothing seemed to go right. I do not know what the problems were, but any minister's schedule is partly unplanned. Last minute hospital visits, elders who wanted to have their plans for the next three weeks approved, problems with getting six people completely packed, etc., probably each played its part, but a planned early morning departure had not yet occurred by mid-afternoon. Dad suggested that we should postpone our departure until the next morning, but Mother, wise in these ways, demurred. "Let's get started," she said, "even if we only go a few miles. If we wait until tomorrow, we will find more things to delay us." And so off we went for forty miles and stayed that night in the small Iowa town of Carroll.

My excitement built as we crossed the Missouri River and into Nebraska. I knew the route we would be taking. I had pored over maps and traced our planned itinerary. We were going to be traveling US Highway 30 all the way from Boone to San Francisco. To my somewhat foreshortened vision Nebraska was THE WEST. It was, however, a somewhat disappointing and flat West. I knew that Nebraska didn't have mountains, but surely it at least had deserts and buffalo and, most importantly, buffalo **skulls** lying about on the western prairie waiting to be picked up. Sad to say we never saw one buffalo or even a buffalo skull, We did, however, see some very dry and dusty land that served in my eleven-year-old imagination as desert in western Nebraska.

Despite my disappointment with Nebraska, we soon rolled into Wyoming, which I **knew** was part of the true West. Here, I was not disappointed. As we rolled across southern Wyoming, ahead we began to see what looked at first like clouds hanging on the horizon, but were soon revealed as mountains. I was seeing my FIRST REAL MOUNTAINS, and I was in heaven. I had read about them, I had dreamed about them. But here was the REAL THING! I remember the excitement I felt but I don't remember a great deal of detail about that day. I do remember that dad was somewhat concerned about how his car would behave pulling a trailer over the mountains.[4] His worries were justified. More than once we had to pull over to the side of the highway and give the overheated liquid in the radiator a chance to cool. These were great opportunities for Bill and me, because it gave us time to explore.

When we could, we stayed at a trailer park, but there were not many of them and often there was not one where we wanted to stop. We sometimes requested permission of a local service station to set up behind their building. This was advantageous because they usually had an outdoor water tap available. I would guess we probably stopped in Grand Island, and probably Cheyenne, but I don't know.

---

[4]In 1948 there were no Interstates with their smooth and gentle ascents and descents carved out of the mountains. Highway 30 literally went up and over the high passes, sometimes at a very steep grade.

They were virtually the only large towns along our route.[5] But after we left Cheyenne there were no towns of any size at all clear across Wyoming and Utah until we reached Salt Lake City. We spent several nights both going out and coming back, simply camped along the side of the road, wherever we could find a suitable place. I doubt whether we would be allowed to do that today.

I remember one night when we camped along the road like that. It was a rather chilly evening, so we ate inside the trailer. Eating inside was very cramped with the six of us, so when I finished eating, I decided to go outside for a while. (I might also have had the notion that this would get me out of helping with the cleanup. It probably didn't). I was doing nothing but wandering around, enjoying the feeling of complete isolation, knowing that aside from my family there was probably no one around for many miles, when suddenly there was a bright light which lit up the sky in the west. It was rising over the horizon, and majestically crossed over the sky from west to east. When it got low in the east, it suddenly disappeared. I was mesmerized. I had never before seen such a bright light in the night sky (I still haven't seen anything else like it to this day). I was certain at the time that it was a very large meteor, and it very probably was, but I have wondered since whether I had actually seen a UFO. Of course I had (and have) no way of proving it one way or the other. My family seemed unimpressed when I told them about it, but then none of them had seen it. It is however "emblazoned" on my memory to

____

[5]Cheyenne was not actually very big, about 7000 at that time, despite being the capital of Wyoming.

this day.

I have no memory of Salt Lake City, except for the breath-taking view of it when we first came out of the mountain pass and could see it all spread out below us. I suspect that this may have been the pass-through which Brigham Young crossed when he proclaimed, "This is the place." I do, however, remember the Great Salt Desert immediately to the west of the city. This was perhaps the first of the great western landmarks which I had read about and anxiously anticipated seeing.

After we passed Salt Lake City and the Great Salt Desert, we faced the endless drive across the entire width of Nevada, which was very arid, and much of it desert, with no towns at all for its entire width. I may have gotten bored, but my memory is of continuous excitement, and an endless thrill each time we saw something new. I remember particularly at one point as we were driving across Nevada, a small herd of pronghorn antelope, perhaps seven or eight, suddenly appeared out of nowhere and raced us right alongside the car for perhaps a mile or two and then speeded up, crossed the road in front of us and disappeared into the distance. Talk about getting excited! I can still see them vividly to this day, and feel the thrill which I felt then.

After spending a night in Reno, we drove into California, past the spectacular Lake Tahoe, and through another mountain range. By this time that was becoming old-hat and I, at any rate, was getting impatient to get to San Francisco, which I had read a lot about.

One of the first things we discovered when we got to San

Francisco was that the city did not permit trailer parks in the city limits. That, however, was Dad's problem, not mine. After making inquiries, Dad discovered a trailer park on the eastern shore of the bay in the small town of Brisbane. I have vivid memories of Brisbane. It resembled to me at the time nothing so much as a small Mediterranean town, with small houses built into the side of the hill like stairsteps, and all a brilliant sun-washed white. Even at ten years old, I had seen pictures of such towns and was fascinated, I might say charmed, by the appearance of the town. It was right on the bayside, and we had a view of the giant freighters and sea-going tankers as they came and went to their moorings. To me the whole setting was truly exotic.

Although I was charmed, I am sure Dad was vexed that he had to park the trailer so far from the city and was forced each morning to drive through rush hour traffic and across the Bay Bridge to get to the site of the convention. I remember visiting the convention hall once during the week, but about all I remember was a vast hall, filled with several thousand persons. I really don't remember how Bill and I spent most of that week, and now that I think about it that is a little odd. Dad took some time off from the convention for family sightseeing, and we did take one whole day at the end of the convention to see the wonders of San Francisco.

We visited Chinatown, and I remember being somewhat disappointed. I don't know what I expected, but it looked just about like any other business district except that many of the signs were in Chinese. We ate at a small restaurant there which was located on the second floor. That was a novelty for me, but as I remember, I didn't much care for the food. We also visited Fisherman's Wharf, which was more interesting. We ate there also. I remember this in particular because we ate at a restaurant which had windows right beside our table, and they looked out onto the wharf. As we ate, we watched some boys fishing. There was a flock of seagulls flitting about and as one boy cast, a seagull swooped down and grabbed his bait, which would have been funny, except that he got the hook also. We watched as the boy wrestled with the seagull until he got him close enough that he could cut the line and free the bird.

We took the southern route back to Iowa, through southern California, Arizona, and New Mexico. We spent an entire day in Yosemite National Park, which in many ways was the high point of the trip for me. We saw all the famous sights—Half Dome, El Capitan, Bridal Veil Falls, and of course, the mighty redwoods, some of the largest and oldest living things on earth. The sight of them was awe-inspiring, and for one ten-year-old boy, a sight never to be forgotten. Many years later, when I visited the Muir Woods north of San Francisco, I realized that the sequoias there could be even taller and wider in diameter than the Redwoods of Yosemite. But at that time, and still today in retrospect, those redwoods were awesome! One of the most famous sights in the park was the living redwood which had had a road cut right through it wide enough for cars to drive through. What seemed marvelous then, I now see as a sacrilege, a blasphemy against the majesty of God's handiwork. But at the time, it was just amazing and wonderful!

The original plan had been to stop and see the Grand Canyon and I was eagerly anticipating that. But Dad announced that we were running out of time, and we would have to skip that. I proceeded to make everyone in the car miserable for about two days, whining "Why can't we see it?"

Crossing through northeastern New Mexico and southwestern Kansas, we ran into a terrific dust storm, which made it almost impossible for dad to see the road. For me, that was a great bonus. I had read about such phenomena and here I was experiencing one firsthand! For Dad, not so much.

Such was the great adventure of my childhood.

VI.

BULLIES CAN BE BEATEN (BUT IT'S PAINFUL)

Let me say it up front. I am a wimp—always have been and always will be. As a child, this made me vulnerable to bullying. From kindergarten, when Terry Joe Whittaker made my life miserable, through junior high, I suffered through a series of bullies who, for whatever reason, seemed to delight in tormenting me. Summer vacation would usually provide some relief, but even then I couldn't always avoid them.

The occasion that I recall took place one summer evening when I was about thirteen. I was hanging out one evening in the neighborhood with two of my friends, both of whom were a year or two younger than I was, doing nothing much and enjoying it greatly, when we were joined by Eddie, an older boy whom I knew slightly, but had never had real trouble with before. Our wanderings took us to the city park, where there was plenty of scope for our imagination. However, what had started out as a typical pleasant summer evening turned sour when Eddie began to taunt me.

I tried to ignore him, but he sensed red meat, and he bored right in. Eventually he called me a coward and said I was afraid to fight him (he got that right!). But for some reason, which to this day I don't understand, this stuck in my craw. "I'm not afraid. I just don't want to fight," I said. But he wasn't buying any of that. He kept up the taunt, until I said, "All right. I **will** fight you."

Understand—I **never** fought voluntarily. I got beat up

occasionally, but not since a drubbing at the hands of Terry Joe Whittaker had I voluntarily entered into a fight. I never liked the feeling of being someone else's punching bag. Eddie was several inches taller than I was, and probably outweighed me by thirty pounds. At that moment he looked like Goliath to my David, except I didn't have a slingshot. But I was committed now, and there was no choice but to wade in. Of course I was hopelessly outmatched. Pretty soon I wasn't trying to throw punches. I was too busy trying to protect myself. Eddie paused and said, "Do you give?" My proper response was "Yes", but something in me wouldn't let me utter that word. All I could gasp out was "No". The punishment proceeded. Pretty soon he had me up against a tree and was pummeling me for all he was worth. "Say uncle!" "No." The pummeling continued. Soon I was jelly on the ground, but I still couldn't utter the word of surrender. Why? I honestly don't know. Some shred of self-respect must have sealed my lips. After a while, Eddie just quit in disgust. I guess it stopped being fun.

And then a miraculous thing happened! My two friends who had been watching all this take place, now stepped in. To Eddie they said "Go away. We don't want to play with you anymore." And then they began to tell me how brave I was, standing up to a bully like that. The rest of the evening, I was King of the Walk (albeit pretty sore). They treated me like I was a hero. I knew I wasn't, but I sure liked the feeling. I think I gained some self-respect that night, and I know I gained a lot of self-confidence.

I would like to report that that was the last time I suffered from bullies, but of course it wasn't. It was not until we moved from Boone, Iowa to Bloomington, Illinois that I finally shook the image as a ready mark for bullies. I remember talking with my mother about the proposed move, and saying, "I think that in a new place and in a new school, I can start over again." And sure enough, it worked. But I wonder, would it have worked if I hadn't already proved to myself that I didn't have to knuckle under to Eddie?

VII

HOW I MET YOUR MOTHER

My nephew Ric Hudson's wife Joyce Vann has an interesting hobby. She collects accounts of how married couples met each other. The interesting thing about this hobby, she says, is that most of the time the husband and wife tell different stories. This is certainly true of Kay and me. Our two stories bear no resemblance to each other. What I here recount is of course, the **true** story.

Each fall at the start of the new school year, Drake University had an Orientation Week for new freshmen and transfer students. Each day of the week covered a different aspect of student life. One (Thursday, I think) was devoted to Religion on Campus, which consisted of short speeches by various college officials and an introduction of the campus ministers. This was followed by parties given by each student religious organization in their respective churches.

In the fall of 1957 Dale Miller, head of the Religion Department, asked several of his students to prepare a dramatic introduction to the evening's program. Among others, he asked me to help out. I forget who else was on the committee, except for Myron Talcott, who was a close friend (and who served as my best man at our wedding). Myron was an earnest fellow, who took this assignment very seriously and instilled in us a desire to produce something truly worthy of the occasion. Consequently we worked long and hard on the program, and being who we were (bright, earnest, young and creative), we

25

produced a program which I am still proud of to this day.

The program went off splendidly. Dr. Miller was impressed. Each of us on the committee no doubt thought of ourselves more highly than we ought (I know I did). But then it was On To The Party!

The party for those of the Christian Church persuasion was held in the University Christian Church, right across the street from Old Main, the campus building in which the first part of the evening had been held. As I recall, there was quite a large crowd there. As the principle purpose of such a party was to get acquainted, and to make the new students feel at home, those of us who were members of the Disciples Student Fellowship were expected to circulate, engage the visitors in conversation and try to make everyone feel at home.

But a subsidiary (sub rosa?) purpose of most of the young males in attendance was to scout out the new girls. I remember standing on a sort of balcony overlooking the large party hall and talking to Ian McRae, the Disciples campus minister, when I spotted this really attractive and vivacious girl who was just sitting down at the piano. "Now there's someone I would like to get to know," I thought to myself. So as soon as I could excuse myself, I drifted over to the piano where this girl was playing very confidently and from memory all sorts of popular songs of the day. She had gathered quite a crowd around the piano, so it took me some while to get close. Just as I got near the piano, this really handsome guy came in from the kitchen where he had apparently gone to find a couple of wooden spoons to use as a percussion accompaniment to her piano. They conversed and laughed together in a relaxed familiar way that spoke of long acquaintance. Then they began playing together, she on the piano, and he on the wooden spoons. "Darn," I thought. "All the good ones are already taken." By the end of the party I still had not had an opportunity to speak with her, but she had made a big impression on me.

I didn't give a lot of thought to this until I met her on campus a week or so later. (Her account of how we met would begin here.) It seems that we had both signed up for a class on evolution. When we arrived at the class, however, we discovered that we were the only two to sign up for that particular class, and so it was canceled. This gave me an opportunity to get acquainted with her as we walked together to the Registrar's office to change our classes. We both switched to a class on genetics, taught by Dr. Fae Shawhan, a kindly looking grandmotherly type, who, however, was as demanding as any professor I had in my four years at Drake.

During our walk, and subsequent cup of coffee, we discovered that we both had the same advisor, and were both majoring in religion. In the course of our conversation, I casually mentioned that I had seen her at the Disciples' party the previous week with her boyfriend. At that she laughed and said, "That was my twin brother." That certainly explained a lot about why they were so comfortable with each other. I don't remember whether I asked her for a date then or later, but it was at that point that I decided to ask at some time.

These things are seldom smooth, however. The next week I attended a concert by myself, and who should be sitting at the other end of the same row—this luscious and desirable girl with a lordly upper class pre-medical student. I figured that she had found better male companionship, and that I was out in the cold. I'm not quite sure exactly how that was resolved, but somehow or other she let me know that she did indeed enjoy my company, and soon we were dating in earnest.[6]

Then there was a friend. We will just call him Bill, a really nice guy whom we still see occasionally. Bill was a senior and also a religion major, and at that age he was supremely self-confident and more than a little arrogant. It never occurred to him that he couldn't get about anything he wanted. One day he announced to all and sundry, that Kay was his girl, and everybody else should just lay off. By that time, Kay and I had been dating for long enough that I recognized this for the hot air it was, and I totally ignored him. I never noticed that my impinging on his self-declared territory had any negative impact on our friendship.

And finally there was Dwight (see my anecdote titled **Pat**). Dwight was also a junior transfer student, as was Kay, and he was also much taken with Kay. That first fall, there were retreats being held for Disciples students on successive weekends at Lake Aquabi, a state park perhaps thirty miles from Des Moines. On each of these weekends, Dwight offered Kay a ride to the retreat, and each time she accepted. However, both times she changed her mind, when I asked her to ride with me. For a long time, Dwight accused me of doing this deliberately, but both times, it was entirely Kay's decision. I didn't

---

[6]Years later, this same medical student, then a successful doctor, became famous as the father of the Beverly Hills Madam, Procurer for the Stars. I would modestly suggest that Kay lucked out.

know until much later about his offers of a ride. I do believe, however, that I made amends to him a year or so later, when I introduced him to Pat. You have by now undoubtedly read far more than you wanted to know about how I met your mother. Live with it.

VIII

**NEVER LIE TO YOUR WIFE (EVEN IF YOU'RE NOT
MARRIED YET)**

What I am about to tell you is one of the oddest experiences I have ever had. I have no explanation for it, but I assure you it really happened.

Kay and I met in the fall of 1957 at the start of the school year. We were soon dating exclusively, and by the start of Christmas vacation we were engaged, although few people knew it at the time. Kay planned to go home to Columbia, Missouri for the holidays. I had to stay in Des Moines because, among other reasons, I had a part-time job. We agreed that I would drive down to Columbia on the weekend before classes were to resume and bring her back to Des Moines. (That trip, by the way, was one of the most harrowing I ever took, but that is another story.)

During the period of time that Kay was in Columbia, as I was riding home on the bus from my down-town job, I met Margaret Hellie, whom I had dated extensively for two years before she left to attend Vassar. Margaret was the only other girl I had ever been serious about, and we were still good friends. I was delighted to see her, and we spent the time on the bus ride catching up on each other. When we got to my stop, I stayed on with her until her stop. We then went to her house where we spent a couple of hours talking and enjoying each other's company. I showed her Kay's picture and told here we were engaged. After that I went home and did not see her again during the

30

Christmas break.

Let me be clear about one thing. I was committed to Kay (still am) and deliriously happy that she had agreed to marry me. Still, I felt slightly uncomfortable about spending time enjoying the company of an old girlfriend. So meeting Margaret was a matter that I deliberately and self-consciously did *not* tell Kay when she came back to Des Moines.

It must have been a couple of months later that Margaret's name came up in conversation. I'm not quite sure how this happened, because for aforementioned reasons I was reluctant to talk to her about former girlfriends, particularly Margaret. Kay's response was surprising. "Is that the girl you introduced me to on the bus?"

My first reaction was confusion and bewilderment. When had I ever introduced Kay to Margaret? Then I realized that it would have been impossible, because the two of them had never both been in town at the same time. I had seen Margaret one time since I had met Kay, but that could not be the time. Still, it *was* on a bus. Curious and a little spooked, I began to question Kay.

"Describe her to me."

"She had strawberry blonde hair." Right!

"What color were her eyes?"

"Blue." Right again! But blonde hair and blue eyes often go together, and that could be a shrewd guess.

"What color coat did she have on?"

"Red." Still right! About now I am beginning to get seriously spooked!

"What seat was she sitting in?" She told me, and she was exactly right! Yikes!

I was about to question her some more, but she cut me off and told me she didn't want to talk about it anymore, so we dropped it. Many years later she told me that as soon as I began to question her, she realized that nothing like this had ever happened, and she started to get scared too.

Years later I ran into Margaret when we were living in Chicago. Margaret at that time was teaching at the Illinois Institute of Technology. We didn't have much time to talk, but I told her of this incident. She was totally skeptical. "You must have told her about me and then forgot about it," she said.

Well, maybe. But as I have already mentioned, I deliberately intended **not** to tell Kay about it, and if I did would I likely forget that I had? Besides, would I have described everything to her in detail? Possibly. She is a strawberry blonde with blue eyes. But why would I have told her the color of the coat she was wearing? And most of all, why would I have told her which seat she was sitting in?

I don't know what you would do in such a circumstance, but I *never* lie to Kay.

P.S. I also told her of my meeting with Margaret in Chicago. Never take chances.

IX

A DEMONSTRATION IN DES MOINES

My years at Drake University were by and large a wonderful experience. Intellectually, socially and in every other way they were for me a time of real growth. I don't even regret the time I joined a "mob". In retrospect I learned a lot about myself, and about how easy it is to lose oneself into a herd mentality.

To understand what happened requires a bit of background. Drake at that time had a tradition of declaring an officially sanctioned "Skip Day" one Monday in the fall following a big football victory, when all classes were canceled. It was looked forward to by most students, even those who could care less about football.

Unfortunately, 1957 was a very bad year for Drake football. They lost game after game. It came close to the end of the season and the team had yet to notch a significant win. The administration, in its wisdom (and no doubt pushed by student leaders) decided to announce a Skip Day even without the football victory. It was suitably declared and enjoyed by all students. The next weekend was the final game of the season, against Iowa State. Iowa State's football program was hardly stellar, but they played a level of football well above that of Drake, and no one expected anything other than another drubbing.

The night of the game was miserable. The temperature hovered around 30 degrees, a chilly wind was blowing, and it spat snow and sleet most of the game. I attended the game—I guess out of a sense of duty. I was that way in those days. Moreover, I stayed for the entire game. Generously speaking, there might have been a few hundred students in attendance, and many of those hardy souls left at halftime. They were much smarter than me. At the end of the game I could barely stand up. My knees were nearly frozen in place. Nevertheless I was exultant. I had witnessed a miracle. Drake had beaten Iowa State!

That would be the end of it, and this would be a non-story except for one thing. The following Monday morning a group of students decided that after such a glorious victory we needed a Skip Day. No matter that we had already had one a week earlier. A rare win over Iowa State **demanded** a special celebration.

Soon the rumor was spreading over the campus. This was to be a Skip Day! Some of the leaders of this impromptu celebration began going around to classrooms encouraging students to cut class and join the celebration. Some professors went along and canceled class. Others refused and warned students that if they left, they would be counted absent and that this could affect their grade. Soon a sizable crowd of several hundred or more students gathered outside of Old Main. This crowd consisted of maybe ten times as many students as had actually attended the game, but no matter. A principle was at stake. A great victory required a Skip Day.

I was in that crowd, as excited as anyone else, but not entirely unaware of the discrepancy in the makeup of the crowd on Monday morning and the one on Friday night. We called for President Harmon to come out and declare the Skip Day official. Instead, some junior administrator came out and explained what we all already knew. We had had a Skip Day already, and could have only one each fall. He advised us to return to our classes, not a big seller with this crowd.

Finding we were making no progress with the president, someone suggested that we should take our demand to the governor. I have no idea who came up with this brilliant idea, but it seemed to make sense to us at the time. So, maybe 1000 or more strong, we proceeded to march down University Avenue, along Keo Way, on Grand Avenue through the heart of downtown, across the Des Moines River and up Capitol Hill, shouting and chanting along the way. Along about the time we turned onto Keo Way, the police showed up. I was mildly surprised that they didn't try to stop us, but instead gave us an escort all the way to the Capitol. In retrospect it was a wise move. We were in a festive mood, but if they had tried to stop us things could have turned ugly. Escorting us kept us, and the citizens of Des Moines, safe.

Once we arrived outside the Capitol building, we commenced shouting for the governor. After a little while, someone (not the governor) came out to talk with us. He was sorry, he said, but the governor was not in his office (surprise, surprise!), but he sympathized with our demands. This official promised that he would contact the president of the University and express our demands. This shrewd response seemed to take the steam out of the mob. I don't even recall that he suggested that we disperse, but that is what happened. We suddenly became aware that we were about five miles from the campus, with no transportation back home. Most of us were tired and hungry by the time we got back. We actually got our "unofficial" Skip Day, but at the cost of spending most of the day demanding it.

Thus ended my only experience in mass civil disobedience, or if you will, mob behavior. In retrospect, the realization how easily supposedly intelligent people (I include myself in that category) could turn into a mindless mob is a little disconcerting. Membership too easily gives a sense of immunity from responsibility. I have since been suspicious of mass behavior of any sort. It may have its uses but can be a dangerous and two-edged sword.

X

PAT

This is really Pat's story, not mine, but since Kay and I played a significant part in it, I trust she will not be offended if I appropriate it.

Pat is one of the strongest and most courageous women I know. From very unpromising beginnings, and with odds stacked against her, she has made a great life for herself. Her family background was not promising. Her parents were, to say the very least, eccentric. Her father ran a used furniture store, which he advertised as being open "Tuesdays and Saturdays and some other days". Pat's mother was a very disturbed woman. She had in her life developed a hatred of all men, and did all she could to inculcate Pat with the same hatred and fear. Pat had had a very distorted childhood and had a fear of men which lasted throughout her teenage years. Consequently, she arrived at the age of twenty-one never having had any friendships or dealings with any boy or man. She and Kay had been friends since high school and attended Christian College together. Pat, however, stayed home under the thumb of her mother when Kay left for Drake University.

Eccentric though he was, her father saw what was happening and urged her to break free of her mother. I do not know what the precipitating factor was, or whether there was indeed any. But one day Pat decided to leave home and strike out on her own. How difficult that decision was I can only guess, but with commendable determination, she simply packed a suitcase, walked out the door and bought a bus ticket to Des Moines. She chose Des Moines because that was the only place where she knew anybody.

When she arrived in Des Moines, she got a room at the YWCA and went job hunting. It was not until she had found a job that she let Kay even know that she was in town. This she did by showing up on her doorstep one afternoon. Kay, of course, was delighted to see her, and when she found out what she was about, urged Pat to move in with her. Kay was at that time living with her Aunt Mary, who had a big old house near the Drake campus and plenty of room for another roomer. Pat and Kay thus became roommates. This ends the first phase of this story.

Part two concerns the dilemma in which this placed Kay and me. Pat was lonely, knowing no one but Kay in Des Moines. Kay and I wanted to try to show her a good time. We invited her to go with us to movies, miniature golf dates, picnics, DSF affairs, and so on. Pat was delighted to have something to do besides sit alone in her room. However, it soon developed that she thought that she had a standing invitation to go with us wherever we went. This was not good. Like most engaged couples, we wanted *some* time alone, without a third party being along. What could we do, without hurting Pat's feelings?

After some deliberation we decided that if we could involve a fourth party (male) in our excursions, which might solve the problem naturally and without any feeling of rejection on Pat's part. How to do this, though, given Pat's fear of males, was a problem that required some subtlety. We accordingly devised a rather elaborate scheme.

Mother had been asking my brother Bill and me to build a picket fence around the back yard all summer. Kay felt that if Pat could meet some nice young man accidentally in the pursuit of some other activity, a friendship might sprout and thus help us to solve our problem. Accordingly I asked my good friend Dwight (currently unattached) if he could help me dig postholes and set posts for the fence the next Saturday. To make this request more plausible, I explained that Bill had promised to help, but that he had other urgent business the next Saturday, and it was really a two-person job. I took Mother into our confidence on the scheme so that she could head Bill off. (That guy was always gung-ho for any job that required hard work. To this day I don't understand it.)

Saturday came. Dwight showed up at 8:00 ready to work. We were soon busily fence-building. By design, about 10:00 Kay said to Pat, "Let's go down and see what Dave is doing," (we were so subtle in those days!). Arriving, they found that (surprise!) I had a stranger (to Pat) working with me. Dwight and I of course welcomed the excuse to stop working and to talk. We introduced the two, and soon there was a lively three-way conversation taking place. Unfortunately that conversation didn't include Pat. She stayed close to Kay and looked uncomfortable.

This wasn't the way we envisioned the encounter going, so to push matters along, I said "Mother has some ice cream in the freezer. Would anyone like some?" Of course the answer was yes, and I asked Kay to help me dish it up. I cleverly figured that if we left Pat and Dwight alone, they would get acquainted better. Kay and I headed for the kitchen. As we reached the back door, we turned around and there was Pat directly behind us! She was not about to be left alone with a strange man!

Of course, we all enjoyed the ice cream, but Kay and I figured our scheme was a failure. So it was with some surprise that a few days later, I encountered Dwight on the campus, and he asked me whether this "intriguing woman of mystery" (my words, not his), was currently dating anyone. I assured him that she was not, and that if he was interested he should give her a call. I do not know details of that conversation, but Pat apparently gathered enough courage to say, "Yes," to Dwight's invitation, and before we knew it, they were spending a lot of time in each other's company. Our problem appeared to be solved. End of phase two. But as they say in those TV infomercials, "But wait, there's more."

Act Three took place some months later in October. Bill and I finally finished the fence before the snow flew, and mother thought we should celebrate. Accordingly, the four of us were enjoying ourselves on a cool night in October, making fudge and playing cards, when there was a knock on the door. Mother went to answer it, and found Pat there. Mother was of course glad to see her, knowing how much Pat had had to do in getting the fence started. "Pat, come on in and join us. We are celebrating getting the fence finished."

At this, Pat collapsed in tears. She had come looking for Kay to tell her that she and Dwight had broken up, and the symbolism of the fence was too much for her. We consoled her as best we could, as friends will do on such tragic occasions. I don't know how consoled Pat felt when she left that night with Kay, but we did our best.

The story was, however, still not over. Dwight and Pat eventually got back together, married and have been a happy pair now for almost sixty years. Dwight became a fine minister, and served churches in Michigan, Iowa, and California. Pat went back to school, earned her degree, taught, and worked as a regional officer in the Disciples' central offices in Michigan and California. They are one of the few couples which we have kept in contact with over the years, and a pair whom I admire greatly.

XI

THE YEAR THE GRINCH ALMOST STOLE OUR CHRISTMAS

The following story was not written by me. It was written by Kay for a Christmas pamphlet put out by our church at Christmastime, 1983. I know that these are supposed to be my anecdotes, but I was as fully involved on this occasion as was Kay. And since she did such a fine job of telling this story, why should I try to retell it?

DH

Christmas 1970 was a lean time for our family. We were living in Chicago where my husband Dave was in graduate school and our children were in grade school. In spite of meager funds, we managed to have a Christmas tree and buy some presents for our children. We looked forward to the special Christmas holidays for our family to spend together. A Christmas Eve service was planned by our small church at the Community Center across the street from our apartment building.

Later Christmas Eve afternoon we took all of our clothes down to the laundry room on the first floor of the building and put them into the washers. Then we went back upstairs and ate our supper while the clothes were washing. Just before we left to go across the street to the Community Center for the Christmas Eve service we took the clothes out of the washers and put them into the dryers. Then we left for the service.

It was a beautiful candlelight service which our tiny church shared that evening. A special symbol was the beautiful Christmas cactus, the "Christmas Rose", which blooms in the dark and cold of winter. As we left to go home, we all felt the special glow that Christmas Eve brings.

On our way upstairs to the apartment, we stopped in the laundry room to pick up the clothes. They were gone! At first we thought we had checked the wrong machines, but further investigation revealed no clothes. All of our clothing, the girls' favorite dresses, were gone, and we knew we couldn't afford to replace them. Our spirits were so low—we couldn't believe that anyone would pick Christmas Eve to steal our belongings. As we talked about it, we became determined that our "Grinch" was not going to spoil our Christmas. After all, was Christmas dependent on the things we own, or on our love for each other? We went upstairs to the apartment, turning on the Christmas tree lights and sat in a circle singing Christmas carols until that warm glow crept back into our hearts. Then we said good night and went to bed.

The next morning we got up early and opened presents and ate breakfast. A little later in the morning one of the girls [Laura] went down to the laundry room. There were all of our clothes back again! *[I must add here just a word. I will never forget Laura running down the hall yelling at the top of her lungs, "They're back! They're back!". Dave]*. Apparently either they had been taken by mistake the night before or someone had second thoughts. We were so happy to get them back.

But we had already learned that material possessions are not what is important about Christmas. People who love each other are!

We never have forgotten the Christmas that was almost stolen by the "Grinch."

XII

THIS OLD HOUSE

I finished course-work for my master's degree at the University of Chicago Library School in the spring of 1971. Although I still had a master's thesis to write, it was time to look for a job. Accordingly, I sent out feelers to more than fifty academic libraries, from the University of Alaska to the University of the Virgin Islands, most of whom had been advertising positions available. I heard back from very few of them, but one which responded positively was the University of Iowa. That possibility seemed almost too good to be true, so I promptly responded. The upshot was the offer of a job as Circulation Librarian at the Main University Library, beginning at the start of school in the fall.

Now that I had a job in Iowa City, the next order of business was to find someplace to move the family to. Accordingly, in July Kay and I went house-hunting. We had had enough of apartment living in Chicago and were definite about finding a house. However, having just finished with graduate school, we were not in any position to buy one. What we hoped to find was a satisfactory house for rent. However, after spending a whole day looking for rental property in and around Iowa City, we came up blank. Houses for rent were almost non-existent. The only one we had found was for rent at a rate far above our pocketbook.

Discouraged, we drove back to Davenport to stay with Mother, who was then living there. Our plan was to return to Iowa City the

45

next day and continue looking. We spent part of that evening visiting with Fran Kirkpatrick, a cousin of Kay's who, with his wife Ruth, lived in nearby Bettendorf. After we had explained our mission and its lack of success thus far, Fran said "Why don't you go back to Iowa City tomorrow and go to church at First Christian? I know the minister there and he is a fine fellow. His name is Bob Welsh. Perhaps he knows of someone in his congregation who has a house available for rent but has not actively advertised it." Since this pretty much agreed with our plans, and since we had no Plan B to pursue, we agreed that that sounded like a good idea.

The next morning we did as Fran had suggested. We were pleasantly surprised that the worship service was much like that of our somewhat offbeat congregation in Chicago. After worship, I approached the minister and introduced myself. I said that we would be moving to Iowa City in August, and—I got no further than that when Bob grabbed my arm and said, "Come over here There is someone I want you to meet." He then introduced us to Dean and Ellen Jones. The first words out of Ellen's mouth—the very first!— were, "Do you want to rent a house?" Now I am not one who believes that God goes around planning every detail of our lives, but there are times in my life when I could almost be persuaded. Of course we wanted to—that was our whole purpose in being here.

After a brief discussion, Dean and Ellen invited us out to dinner (which they insisted on paying for), and then we drove out to Coralville, at that time a small suburb of Iowa City. There they showed us a quaint house which Kay and I both fell in love with before we even saw the interior. It was a 1½ story with a most unusual roof line which almost resembled a thatched roof, although it was of course made of conventional materials. Inside, the house was almost as charming. It had three bedrooms, a large kitchen, and a huge living room, which we discovered later had been made out of two original rooms. This was even better than we had hoped for, and the rent was almost the same that we had been paying for an apartment in Chicago! It was a house that Ellen's brother had built for his bride when they were young, and was now about forty-five years old. The Jones's had had the house on the market for several years but had had no luck in selling it, and were now renting it. All right—maybe God did have a hand in it!

The upshot was that we did rent the house, and spent nearly twenty-five years within its walls. After six years we had accumulated enough money for a down-payment, and became proud owners of our dream house. Dream house?—well—What kind of a dream was I living in, anyway?

As many others have testified in similar circumstances, our dream house transmogrified almost immediately into a money pit. What had seemed minor blemishes in its rental state, became, in our new relationship to it, serious defects that needed to be promptly addressed. The windows leaked, and all 28 of them (yes, 28!) needed to be reglazed. Although I was (and am) known as "Mr. Ten-Thumbs" I actually turned myself into a glazier. Several months and dozens of broken panes later, I had winter-proofed our windows. Climbing all over the house in this pursuit, however, had revealed to me how badly the house needed to be repainted. After a brief glance at what professionals charged for their services, I thought, "How hard can this be?" I bought a ladder, some paint brushes, and a few gallons of paint, and proceeded to find out "how hard this could be." But after two summers of enforced labor (and in the process partially overcoming my fear of heights) I had a gleaming house prepared to withstand Iowa winters (or so I thought.). A wet basement? We don't live in the basement, and we could put up with that. But we did have to replace the furnace (Ouch!).

Then came the winter of 1979 (or was it 1978?—no matter). Fimbulwinter arrived. It began to snow on Thanksgiving Day, and continued with brief intervals until mid-February. The temperature plummeted and stayed down almost the whole time, meaning that there were no periods of melting, as there are usually in Iowa winters. The result was that the snows of November were still there in February, making for record snow piles. Cars tied red flags to their radio antennas so that they could be visible at intersections, where the snow was piled so high that it was otherwise impossible to see and thus anticipate the cross-traffic.

It was then that I discovered another unpleasant fact about our "dream home". Our roof was very old and not very "roofish". It began with ice-dams, a fairly unusual condition which occurs when there is a heavy snowpack with low temperatures over an extended time, so that snow on the roof will not melt—at least from the top down. However, on poorly insulated houses (as was ours) the warmth radiating out of the roof will melt the underlayer of snow, causing it to run, as water, down the slope of the roof until it reaches the eaves. There it freezes again, gradually building up a dam which causes later melt water to back up and under the shingles, and into the interior of the house. This is what happened to us.

This was truly the winter of our discontent. Wallpaper peeled off the walls in our bedroom, the sunroom, and the hallway. The plaster fell in the stairway. It came through the ceiling of our living room and elsewhere, leaving unsightly splotches on the ceiling tiles. I would lie in bed at night listening to the drip-drip-drip of water into buckets, wondering what I was going to do. The fact is that, until spring, there was precious little that I **could** do. I have had bouts of depression from time to time in my life, but this was by far the worst time I can recall. All I could think of was, "Here is the biggest investment of my life, and it's falling down about my ears."

But even winter in Iowa does not last forever. As if to compensate for all the trouble, Ma Nature brought an early spring. But the house was already a shambles. Well, this is what one has insurance for. After consultation with my insurance adjuster, she calculated that the damage to the house was about $15,000. Remember, this was more than forty years ago, when such a figure was real money. Heck I had only paid $36,000 for the place when I bought it only about three years before. But, after all the restoration, the house really did shine. The insurance company did not pay for a new roof, however, arguing that that was simply a matter of seriously delayed upkeep. Not getting a new roof was not an option, so I had to foot the bill for that myself. Another $5000! Which, incidentally, I did not have.

Ah, dear old charming, alluring, and irresistible money pit! You broke my heart, and then you broke my pocketbook! How innocent we were!

XIII

BATS IS BATS (AND WHY I HATE THEM)

There was a time when I benignly loved all of God's critters (except mosquitoes). Dogs, cats, wolves, bears, even rattlesnakes (at a suitable distance) were quite acceptable as co-inhabitants of this, God's wonderful creation. This was before I got really well acquainted with bats.

Our house on Fifth Street in Coralville was a charming house, built in the 1920s, by a builder who built it for himself and his family. When we first saw it, we immediately fell in love with it. It had both charm and eccentricity, and seemed perfectly suited for our family. Without a down-payment (I had just finished graduate school) we could only afford to rent it, even though it was for sale. But after six years, we were able to buy it and we became the proud owners of a 1-1/2 story bungalow. The house immediately metamorphosed from our dream home to a money-pit. Things that had never bothered us when we were renting suddenly seemed to demand repair or replacement. That, however, is another story, not this one (See **This Old House**). What is significant here is that the house was rather loosely built. This was not out of carelessness in building, but by intent in the days before central heating and air conditioning. Being loosely built allowed the house to breathe and prevented the buildup of toxic gases inside.

It also provided convenient access to various of God's creatures who had the poor taste to prefer the company of humans. The most

51

common of these were mice. Having two cats and a dog did help discourage the little furry critters, and they were only a minor inconvenience for many years.

One night in spring in the early 1980s, Kay and I had just retired for the evening, when, after about a half hour, Kay turned to me and said, "There's something in here.". I was about to tell her to go back to sleep, when I felt and heard the rustle of wings, as **something** circled above my head. I turned on the light, and beheld an obviously confused bat, circling the room in what I interpreted as agitation. Aside from my irritation at being awakened I did feel some sympathy for the little creature who had obviously gotten lost and found himself in the wrong place. For my own peace of mind, and for his, I needed to usher him back outdoors, where all such creatures belonged.

We had never before had this problem, and I was uncertain how to corral him. My first efforts with a paper bag were ineffectual, to say the least. The bat's sonar system helped him easily to avoid my clumsy swoops with the bag. I then had an inspiration. I would try my fish landing net. Being open mesh, it would not be as easy for the bat's sonar to detect, and it had a handle, allowing me to extend my reach without losing control. In short order, I had the bat captured, and I carefully took him outdoors and released back into his "proper environment".

Feeling good about myself (I was both defender of the homestead and compassionate toward one of God's critters), I returned to bed. I had just gotten back to sleep, when I was reawakened by the SWOOSH of (I presume) that same bat. Feeling much less compassionate this time, I snared him again, took him outside, and this time executed him. I believe that bats, or at least some species of them, are protected in Iowa, which means that I may have broken the law. If so, so be it. I intended to get a good night's sleep.

Several nights later, we were awakened once again by the SWOOSH of a bat. Thoroughly out of sorts this time, I repeated the procedure of capture and execution. Thus began the summer from Hell. Every few nights, our sleep would be interrupted by bats. Why we were suddenly afflicted with them, after not having had a problem for years I do not know. We searched for their means of entry and found it in the attic, where, once they were under the roof, had chewed their way through the insulation. We tried to block this hole by stuffing it with steel wool, but they just chewed around the blockage.

That summer I learned to hate bats. I now know why they are the familiars of witches, connected with the dark arts, and generally frightful. Until that summer, I believed that bats were as benign as robins. I now know better.

The capstone came one evening in September. We were attending a party at the home of a librarian colleague of mine, Margaret Richardson. There were quite a number of us there and we had been gathered around the piano singing. As the singing trailed off, we got to talking about various things. For some reason, the subject turned to bats, and I recounted my tale of a summer combating them. Margaret laughed and said that she often left her doors open for ventilation on hot summer nights and she had never had any trouble with bats. She had no sooner said this, than I looked up and saw **two** bats flying in through the door. I have never fainted in my life, but I think I came close that time. My legs literally gave way and I fell to the floor. My first thought was, "They've come after me!" Now, I knew even as I thought it that it was ridiculous, but the remarkable coincidence was more than I could take at that moment. I don't remember what happened to the bats, whether they flew back out, or whether some of the guests captured them and ushered them back outside. Come to think of it I don't remember much else that happened that night from that point on. A few glasses of wine may have had something to do with that, however.

Several weeks later while I was at work, one of my colleagues (who had been at the party) asked me if I had seen Margaret recently. I told him that I hadn't. "Well," he said. "She's looking for you. Since the party she has had an infestation of bats, and she blames you!"

XIV

SATURDAY NIGHT IN HIBBING, MINNESOTA IS LIKE
BEING NOWHERE AT ALL

Beginning in the early 1960s, the Hudson clan began a tradition of having a large family reunion every couple of years at a lake in Minnesota. I believe I started it by suggesting that my brothers and I should get together for a fishing trip somewhere in the northland. I was just finishing up graduate school, and I wanted to do something as non-bookish as possible. My brother Lew ran with the idea, found a place to go, and made all arrangements. After the first experience, we all agreed that it was worth repeating. Our wives, however, would have none of this unless they were included. Thus began the series of family gatherings which still continues to this day. Many tales could be told about these gatherings, but this tale took place in the mid-1970s. In fact it's not really about the family gathering at all. That was merely the setting for what is still known today by my daughters as "The Great Hibbing Adventure".

The family gathering that year was held on Lake Kabetogama (near the Canadian border) on an island in the middle of that lake. It was a wonderful time, and we packed up and headed home with a glow of satisfaction for a week well spent. We had not gone more than fifty miles down the road, however, when it became apparent that we had car trouble. The car was beginning to run dangerously hot. Those of you who know northern Minnesota know that there is not a service station on every corner. In fact there are not even any corners, or towns for them to be located in. Most of the northern third of Minnesota is a vast forest with few residents. We were fortunate, however, when, a few miles down the road we found one of those rare service stations. We pulled in, and investigation revealed that we were leaking transmission fluid. Solving the problem would have involved surgery on the guts of the car, but the man at the station replenished the transmission fluid and opined that it would at least get us back home.

He was wrong. By the time we were perhaps twenty miles north of Hibbing, the car started heating again. By the time we were within ten miles of Hibbing, I was convinced that we would never make it even that far without causing serious damage to the car. There were few homes along this stretch of highway. It was mostly unbroken pine forests, but we did come across one small farmhouse. Not having much choice I pulled in to see if I could get any help. A man there was busy at work putting a roof on his garage, but he immediately came down and greeted us. I explained our dilemma, and without hesitation he offered to take me into Hibbing to get some transmission fluid so that we could at least get into town. His wife came out and invited Kay and the girls into the house where she entertained them the whole time her husband and I were gone. When we got into Hibbing, he insisted on helping me find a Chrysler garage (we drove a Plymouth). We found one, but it was closed on Saturday and Sunday. It began to look like we were going to be stuck in Hibbing for the weekend.

When we got back to his house, I discovered that Kay and the girls had been having a wonderful time with his wife. She had even given them a wooden chain cut from a single piece of wood, a piece which her husband had carved. We kept it for many years as a memento of a kind couple who were hospitable in the truest sense of the word.

We made it into Hibbing, got a motel room and spent two of the longest days of our lives waiting for the garage to open. As I recall, there was a horse show nearby which interested Jenny. But for the rest of us, it was television and various other entertainments which we could devise. I taught the girls how to play bridge, but that never took, except with Beth. There was a popular song of the day which was entitled *Saturday Night in Toledo, Ohio is Like Being Nowhere at All.* The girls immediately adopted this as their theme song, with the substitution of Hibbing for Toledo. We had spent almost all of our remaining cash to get the motel room, so we could not afford to go to a restaurant, and we had to scrounge through the remains of our supplies from the week on the island in order to eat. I don't know about the girls, but I remember vividly, and without the least pleasure, canned peas, and corn.

I was up early Monday morning, anxious to get the car into the garage and get it fixed as fast as possible. Of course it wouldn't start, but I had rather expected that. I got it towed in and the problem diagnosed. It was a blown seal, which would require several hours to repair, and the cost was $80. That was a lot of money in those days, but it didn't worry me too much because I had a Mastercard (then called Master Charge). We had already discovered that bank cards were not much in use in Hibbing, so it didn't surprise me when the garage said that they didn't accept them. That was all right. I would just go to the nearest bank and borrow the necessary cash. After all, they are called "bank cards", aren't they?

After finding out where the nearest bank was, I proceeded on with plan B. I walked into the bank and confidently told the nearest teller that I would like to borrow $80 on my Mastercard. "I'm sorry sir," he said, "but we don't handle bank cards." Oops. On to Plan C. "Can you tell me what bank in Hibbing does handle them?" I asked. "I'm sorry, sir, but none of them do," he replied. So much for plan C. The problem was, I didn't have a Plan D. I believe it was about then that I began to sweat. A problem which had turned into a major roadblock was threatening to become a full-blown catastrophe.

At this point another teller at the adjacent desk spoke up. " I believe that I read in the paper last week that Bank X was going to start honoring bank cards today," he said. **Salvation!** I quickly asked directions as to the whereabouts of Bank X and was soon back on quest.

I walked into the second bank with a good deal more uncertainty than I had the first. Suppose the information was incorrect? What would I do then? Nothing practical suggested itself to me.

"Excuse me, sir," I said with some trepidation. "Do you accept Mastercards?" The teller looked confused, and said he wasn't certain. He then turned and walked into a nearby office, where I assumed his superior was ensconced. A few minutes later he came back, this time with another person. Instead of coming directly back to the teller's cage, they began rummaging around in shelves and cabinets. Finally they found what they were looking for, and the teller returned triumphantly with a Mastercard charge slip. He and his supervisor figured out how to use it and I was finally able to borrow my $80!

All was well. The car was soon fixed. I paid for the repairs, and we safely returned to Iowa without further incident. I will say this, though. I am certain that I was the first person ever to use a Mastercard in Hibbing, Minnesota. Considering the sparsity of the northern Minnesota population, I may have been the first to use it in all of northern Minnesota!

XV

ISLAND OF PARADISE

One of the resorts at which the family gathered in the early years of the fishing reunion is still remembered by some of us fondly as the "Island of Paradise". It was Pine Island, an island in the middle of Lake Kabetogama, just south of the Canadian border in Minnesota. This was the first resort at which the entire family gathered, and where many of the traditions which have lasted through the years were formed. The island was about half an hour from the landing by motor launch and was one of only two resorts which existed on the entire lake, which was about forty miles in length. It was truly a wilderness resort. For many of us it was the ideal place to spend the week.

Except for mother, Aunt Carol, Aunt Grace, and Uncle Stan, we were all young, and with young families and adventurous spirits. The excuse for being there was fishing, but most of us in this fish-crazy family felt it was a special place, and not just because there were fish to be caught. The scenery was spectacular and unspoiled, with almost no evidence there had ever been human occupancy, as for the most part there had not been. For those of us with a historical bent, it was fascinating that this had been part of the fur-traders' route to and from the fur country two or three hundred years ago. The voyageurs, however, left little evidence of their passage through.

Walleyes there were aplenty, but they were not easy to catch with the techniques which we employed in more southern waters when we first arrived. The owner of the resort, Maynard Manzke, watched us for two or three days, and then took pity on us. "Look," he said, "let me show how to catch walleyes on this lake." He had a large pontoon boat onto which he loaded most of us and took us across the lake to a place called Mud Bay, a much more beautiful place than its name would indicate. There he proceeded to give us lessons in how to rig lines, and how to present them. Pretty soon we were catching walleyes hand over fist, none of them large, but plenty large enough for us to begin to get really excited. After about an hour the fish suddenly stopped biting. We continued to fish for another half hour, and were just about ready to quit, when I had a bite. This was a fish with authority, and I got over-excited. I guess everybody else did too, because I was given advice left and right. Despite all of the help, I did manage to land the fish, which proved to be a three-pound northern pike. "Aha," said Maynard. "That is why the fish stopped biting. This boy moved in." Sure enough, walleyes were soon biting again. When we left Mud Bay, everyone on the pontoon had their limit of walleyes. Only one other time in all my years of fishing for walleyes do I remember catching them in such abundance and with such ease. That was on Rainy Lake a few years later, while on another family fishing vacation. But each tale in its time and place—

There were many memorable occasions which took place on Pine Island. This was the site of one of my greatest feats of fishing. My brother Bob and I were fishing in Mud Bay. We had anchored and were enjoying being in such a pristine place. Fishing was just the cherry on top, so to speak. We had caught a few mediocre-sized walleye, but nothing particularly exciting. Suddenly I felt a strike, and tried to set the hook. By the response, I knew at once that I had caught something extraordinary. This was no ordinary fish. Each time I tried to gain some line, the fish would give a bit and then pull right back out. It was so powerful that it even moved the boat. As you can imagine, I was very excited. For ten minutes I fought this big catch with everything I had, but made no progress. The harder I reeled the line, the harder it pulled back. Suddenly, after about ten minutes of this struggle, I had a revelation! Looking at the angle of the line relative to our anchor rope, I suddenly realized that I was probably hooked into the anchor rope, and the anchor was reacting to my efforts just as a lunker fish might. I told Bob to pull in the anchor, and sure enough, here was my hook, firmly set in the rope! This has become widely known in family lore as "the day Dave caught the anchor rope". Nevertheless, I will insist to my dying day that this was the most exciting fishing experience I ever had. (Well, it was, until the day many years later that I caught a ten-pound carp!)

Then there was the time when my sister Beth offered to cook up a big batch of Tennessee jambalaya if the kids could catch enough crawdads, the essential ingredient. There were about sixteen children on the island of sufficient age to partake in this effort, and an energetic two evenings were spent devising ways, new and old, to catch the crawdaddies, which were plentiful along the shore and in the shallows around the island. They were able to capture several hundred of them, which was plenty for Beth's exotic (to us mid-westerners) dish, but what the kids hadn't counted on was that each one had to be shelled by hand. They were drafted for that tedious task, but I didn't hear one of them complain. The result was a novelty dish for us all, and it was delicious.

My third oldest nephew, Ric (Dick's son), was scheduled to graduate from high school on the same week as one of the trips to Pine Island was scheduled. He opted to skip his graduation in order to be able to go with the family. We honored his decision by giving him our own graduation ceremony, complete with a guitar processional through an arch of honor. The arch consisted of each of us holding up crossed fishing rods for him to walk under. My brother Lew, never without something to say, provided the graduation speech (albeit somewhat shorter than most of the breed). Pictures exist of this ceremony, including some with Ric "walking on water." He had found some rocks just submerged off the shore, and gave a pretty good imitation of Jesus walking on the water, complete with graduation robe and scraggly beard.

The lake was filled with small and medium-sized islands, which was both pleasing to the eye and gave plenty of protected places to fish, should the wind be blowing in the wrong direction. Pine Island itself was about one hundred acres in size and was entirely wilderness except for the small area which contained the resort. Those so inclined enjoyed hiking around the island and I was one of them. I discovered on the opposite side of the island a charming and peaceful grove of fragrant cedar trees which encompassed a small secluded rocky point. On my trips to Pine Island, I more than once went out to this little sanctuary simply to sit and meditate. I was already in love with the north country, but sitting in this grove, I think I began to sense the soul of the land. In any case whenever I was there, I was at peace.

In the early 1970s, the United States government recognized the special worth of this country when they included it in the new Voyageurs National Park. We were glad to know this because we knew this meant that the particular character of the land would be forever protected. Businesses like the Pine Island Resort were grandfathered in. That is, they could remain open as long as they wished, but when they closed, they could only sell to the National Park Service, and no new business could come in. In this way, the government could be fair to current business owners, but still control the wildness of the place.

In 1976, on the last day of the vacation, my fourteen-year-old daughter Laura came to me and asked me to listen to a song she had just written. We sat down and she played on the guitar and sang her new song "Island of Paradise". By the time she had finished I was in tears. It captured for me the essentials of how I felt about the island and its natural beauty. I was bothered by only one line, but paid it little attention at the time. The line was "Island of Paradise, I'll see you no more." Little did I know. Scarcely a month after we left Pine Island, a tornado destroyed the resort, and Maynard was forbidden by the National Park Service to rebuild. Laura in some way had sensed this. Don't ask me how, but we would indeed "see you no more." Since that time, this song has become something of an unofficial theme song for the family among those of us who were privileged to visit there for several years, but I suspect that it means little to the younger generations of the family. Today if you are boating on Lake Kabetogama you cannot even set foot on Pine Island. It has been declared a bird sanctuary, I believe because ospreys nest there.

I still miss my "Island of Paradise". My one comfort is that it will remain pristine.

ISLAND OF PARADISE

Island of paradise, home of my dreams,
Land of the blue lake, so calm and serene,
Now that I've met you, I'll let you know,
Island of paradise, I hate to go.

Island of paradise, love you so well
When will I see you again? Hard to tell,
But now that I've found you, I want you to know,
Island of paradise, I won't let you go.

Island of paradise, waves on the shore,
After this last day I'll see you no more,
But even away from you, I'll always know,
Island of paradise, I won't let you go.
Island of paradise, I won't let you go.

LAURA HUDSON KITTRELL

XVI

INVENTING A NEW FISHING TECHNIQUE

From time to time in these anecdotes, I have mentioned the family fishing vacations. To actually write about them is somewhat daunting. Where shall I begin? More to the point, where shall I end? From their inception, they have sprawled out across fifty years and countless incidents. What can I say about them without becoming endless? Well, I will try. This may not be the last tale I tell of these family vacations, but this, for me, was certainly one of the most memorable.

The whole idea of extended family fishing vacations actually began with me, although I did not realize at the time what I was starting. It was 1963. I was just finishing graduate school, and I wanted to do something as far away from books and education as possible. For anyone in this family, the answer would be obvious— fishing! I wrote to my brothers via our round-robin letter and suggested that we should get together for a fishing trip, probably in Minnesota. It never even occurred to me that this would be anything but a one-time adult only male trip. My brothers were enthusiastic, but several of them insisted that we include their sons—six of them, aged six to fourteen. Heck, why not?

My brother Lew ran with the idea, and being a Minnesota resident, took it on himself to find a suitable resort and make all the arrangements. The whole thing was a huge success, and we all agreed that we should repeat it. The distaff side of the family, however, said,

"Not so fast. If this happens again it must include the entire family—otherwise, no way." The entire family at this juncture included thirty-two souls, thirteen adults and nineteen children. We were—and are—a prolific family. If, as happened, various uncles, aunts, and cousins were included we were talking about taking over an entire resort for a week. It all sounded like a great idea, and so the biennial family fishing vacation began, and has continued to this day.

After the initial trip to Elbow Lake in Minnesota, the next several vacations took place on Pine Island, a resort on an island in the middle of Lake Kabetogama, just south of the Canadian border, a resort still known among many of us as the "Island of Paradise". Then several vacations were held on Rainy Lake, actually on the Canadian border. The story of some of the guide-led trips into Canadian waters would be worth telling—maybe another time.

For at least the last thirty years the vacations have been held on Gull Lake, near Brainard, Minnesota. In between, however, were two vacations which were held in Tennessee, at Center Point Lake, and it is one of these that this extended introduction is a wordy lead into.

The switch to Tennessee was an attempt to accommodate our sister Beth and our brother-in-law Bill Insel, who lived in Murfreesboro, Tennessee. The lake and surrounding scenery were beautiful, and the resort was quite nice, if a bit up-and-downy (it was built into the side of steep hill). The fishing, however, was terrible. I was not privy to the discussions which moved the vacation back to Minnesota, but I am convinced that this was the motivating factor. You can put up with anything on a fishing vacation except lack of fish!

In any case, on one of these trips to Tennessee, I found myself fishing one day with my uncle Stan Mahannah and my brother-in-law Bill Insel. We had tried several spots in this large lake, but with no success. Finally, Bill suggested a spot where he assured us one could almost always find fish. It was a spot where an almost perpendicular cliff rose up out of the water. The depth three feet off the cliff was at least twenty feet. We pulled up to the cliff and tied off to a tree growing there precariously.

Now I am not a good swimmer and when in a boat I always wear a life jacket. I have never needed it in all my years of fishing, not even in the windstorm we once ran into on Rainy Lake. However, this was a very hot day, and we were securely tied up to the shore. This once I decided to shed my life jacket—the only time, I assure you, that I have ever done so.

Tennessee game laws allow you to fish with more than one line at a time. Bill was thus prepared and got out three poles. The first he baited and dropped off the side of the boat, then turned his attention to another one. I was just baiting my line, when I noticed his pole start to move toward the edge of the boat. Obviously, he had already caught a fish, and one big enough that Bill was about to lose his pole. His back was to the pole and by the time he turned around it would be gone. Without thinking I made a grab for his pole, but missed. By this time, the pole was in the water, and this is where I made my big mistake. I leaned over the edge of the boat and made another grab for the line. I missed again, and this time, I was so overbalanced that I went into the lake right behind it, making a near-perfect dive. Not only did I not have my life jacket on, but I had on heavy work boots. Finding myself suddenly head down under several feet of water, my first thought was, "So this is how I die!"

But the desire for self-preservation took over. I quickly got my head back above my feet, and broke the surface. I was still close enough to the boat that I grabbed the gunnel (or whatever the edge of a boat is called). About this time Bill and Stan were just realizing what had happened and their first reaction was to laugh. I was highly offended. Here I was on the edge of drowning, and they thought it funny! In fairness to them, what they saw was a very wet me, hanging on to the boat and sputtering. It must have looked pretty comical. After I yelled at them to help me (I don't remember the language I used, but I am sure it was uncharacteristically harsh), Stan began to help me into the boat. If you have ever tried this wearing full fishing gear and heavy boots, all soaking wet, you know it is not easy. Bill, however, still laughing, turned his attention to trying to retrieve my hat, which was floating about ten feet away. "Forget the #$@%%#@ hat and help me. I can't swim," (a slight exaggeration, but accurate enough under the circumstances). After a minute or two (probably the longest two minutes of my life) they managed to get me back into the boat. I had, of course lost my glasses, and as I later discovered, in the process of my dive I had snapped the end off of my best rod.

Stan and Bill were inclined to continue fishing, but I was thoroughly miserable and wanted nothing more than to get back to my cabin. They accommodated me, and thereby left the site that represented almost the only genuine fish bite that anyone in the entire camp experienced all week.

The first order of business, after getting clean and dry clothes on, was to see what I could do about replacing my glasses. Without them, I could barely see past the end of my nose, and there was no way I could drive back to Iowa. Kay drove me into Nashville (about forty miles), where we found an optical shop which was able to make another pair in a couple of hours. Back at the lake, things more or less settled back to normal.

There is a sequel to all of this. Each year, on the last evening of the vacation, the family always has a big picnic, where each family tries to get rid of all the food which they have not used up during the week. This is followed by what we unashamedly call an "awards ceremony". The awards are, for the most part, not for accomplishments, but for the biggest mistakes, misfortunes, or calamities which have occurred during the week. These are mostly ad hoc, depending on what has happened during the week, and each is accompanied by a gag "trophy". But one highly coveted award is "Klutz of the Year", which is awarded at the end of each vacation. This is awarded to the one who, in the judgment of the awards committee, has displayed uncommon maladroitness in a variety of ways during the week. This award was actually created for me back in the years when the vacations took place on Rainy Lake, but that's a story for another time. After I had calmed down and could see the humor in what had happened, I confidently expected to win this award. So it was with considerable surprise when the award went to someone else. I must confess that I was more than a little disappointed that it had not been awarded to me.

My brother Lew, however, who usually emceed these occasions, had other plans for me. The Klutz award was usually the culmination of the awards ceremony. But on this particular occasion, he announced that there was a special award that was to be given. The actions of "this person" had so far exceeded all others in the art of fishing that it called for special recognition. He went on to explain that this person had, by his daring and originality, explored a new method of fishing, actually going after the fish in their own territory. He therefore had a special award which was being given, not for klutziness, but for originality in the sport of fishing. He then presented me with a framed picture which one of my nieces had brought with her with the thought that it might be useful as a trophy for the awards ceremony.

The picture? A boat in a lake containing two fishermen. One of the fishermen is standing on the edge of the boat, obviously trying to land a fish he has hooked. The angle at which he is standing makes it inevitable that within the next five seconds he is going to be in the lake!

God planned this. I am sure of it!

XVII

THIS IS RATTLESNAKE COUNTRY!

My middle daughter Laura is, and always has been, very interested in the environment and its preservation. When looking at colleges, she became very interested in Western Washington University. It may have been partly the romance of distant places, but primarily she was interested because the school had an outstanding program in environmental studies, which at the time she was very interested in studying. Kay and I decided that if she was interested, we might just as well take advantage of it. We could drive her out to look at the school and talk to persons there about the program, and at the same time have a great vacation trip.

We had a great trip, and saw a lot—the South Dakota badlands, Mount Rushmore, the Devil's Tower, the Little Bighorn battlefield, as well as the many spectacular vistas of the high plains and the mountains. We saw a vast prairie dog town, herds of fleet pronghorn antelope, windrows of volcanic ash still lining the highways in Washington from the Mt. St. Helen's eruption more than five years earlier, and much else.

On the way back Laura spotted on the map an historic sight in Montana which she very much wanted to see—an old Indian buffalo jump. It was about fifty miles out of the way, and we were running short of time, but we decided we could take the side trip.

A buffalo jump, for those of you who do not already know, is a site which was used by the Indians as a preferred method of hunting buffalo. When most people think of Indians hunting buffalo (if they ever do) they think of Indians on ponies riding amidst the stampeding herd, and shooting individuals with arrows or stabbing them with spears. This is a product of Hollywood imagination. Indians were more practical, not to mention more concerned about personal safety. While they may have engaged in some form of hunting individual buffalo, the much preferred (and safer!) method was to use a buffalo jump. This consisted of stampeding a herd of buffalo over a convenient bluff or cliff, causing them to fall to their deaths, where they could then be easily butchered, and their meat and hides preserved. This was, of course, a highly wasteful form of hunting, as many more buffalo would be killed than could be utilized by the typical Indian village. But it was also more efficient and safer. These sites can still be seen today, and usually have large deposits of bones at the base of the bluff where the buffalo fell.

When we arrived at the site, it was disappointing. I had expected a small museum, or at least a manned ranger station where we could find out more information about the jump. Instead, all we found was a medium-sized sign telling us mostly what we already knew. However, we were here and took advantage of that to walk around and see what could be seen. The sign did say that in the valley below the jump, "tepee rings" could still be seen. These were rings of stones used to secure the bases of tepees for the village while they were engaged in slaughtering the buffalo. "How interesting", I thought. "I think I'll walk down and see whether I can find any of those."

Kay and Laura, however, were not at all enthusiastic about

leaving the parking lot. Aside from the rather steep descent, they pointed to the prominent sign, which read, **WARNING! This is rattlesnake country!**

"Nonsense," I replied. "How dangerous can it be? See, there is a path that leads down to the valley floor. If it were that dangerous, the Park Service wouldn't build walking paths." And away I went. About two-thirds of the way down, the path petered out, and I realized that this was not a path built by the Park Service, but a trail which had been trampled out by the foolhardy, like me. But having come so far, I was determined to continue and see what I could find. Aside from anything else, the prickly pears were in bloom, and they covered the floor of the valley. It was a lovely sight—especially for a Midwesterner like me who had never before seen massive fields of prickly pears in bloom.

I was wandering around the floor of the valley admiring the prickly pears (but not finding any tepee circles), and taking occasional pictures, when, with startling suddenness, a *very loud* buzzing impinged on my consciousness. Looking up, I saw—not more than five feet in front of me—the largest rattlesnake I had ever seen. I swear, to this day, that the snake was as big around as my thigh. My first reaction—fortunately the right one—was to freeze in my tracks. The snake stared at me for a few seconds, and then, satisfied that I was a harmless idiot, turned and slithered away. Not until I was certain that he was gone, did I move a muscle. My first thought was to check whether the snake had any compadres in the vicinity. After surveying a complete circle around me and determining that there were none, I then called on my high school geometry to determine the absolutely straightest line between my present location and the parking lot. Having made that—very quick—calculation, I headed off at flank speed along that path, going up a quite steep slope with the agility, not to mention the speed, of a goat. Actually, I don't believe I breathed until I was back on the friendly looking gravel.

I never did see the tepee circles, and I am quite satisfied that I never will. My one encounter with a REALLY BIG rattlesnake is enough for one lifetime.

XVIII

DISCIPLINE

My parents grew up and raised their family in an age when physical punishment for misbehavior was considered acceptable. Indeed, the failure to use it was considered weakness or excessive indulgence. The Bible was quoted: "Spare the rod and spoil the child". (I must look that up someday and see whether it really is in the Bible.) As a child, I received my share of spankings, administered by both my father and my mother. Dad usually used his hand, and that stung! Mother's hand was less potent, but she made up for it by using a physical aid, in her case a ping pong paddle. I'm sure that at times I did not feel I deserved the punishment, but I probably did. In any case I grew up under this regime, and do not feel that I was warped in any significant way by the infliction of moderate physical chastisement upon my rear.

Having grown up in this way, and not having given it a lot of thought, I used similar means of discipline on my children when they were small. I might never have given it more thought were it not for an incident when my oldest child, Jenny, was about five years old.

We were living in Lakeville, Indiana at the time. Jenny had been playing outside, and when I called her to come in, she ignored me. Irritated, I went out and instructed her to come in at once. "In a minute," she said, or some such delaying tactic. Getting increasingly frustrated, I walked over to her and said, "Go in the house NOW." Jenny was pretty good at knowing how far she could push me, so she began to head for the house, but not fast enough for me, in my increasing state of anger. I picked up a stick and hit her on the back of her legs to emphasize what I wanted. The stick wasn't very big, and I didn't hit her very hard, but she stopped, turned around and looked up at me with wide shocked eyes. "You HIT me!", she said. This shocked me, too. What had I just done? I had just taken my anger out on a defenseless five-year-old. I don't remember the rest of our interaction on that occasion, but I knew then and there I must never **ever** strike my children in anger again.

I don't think that I spent a lot of time contemplating appropriate forms of punishment for childish misbehavior, but I do know that I always felt uncomfortable when I administered a spanking, no matter what the circumstances. My children grew up, I think, without being unduly warped by it. They are all three admirable adults and caring parents.

Fast forward about thirty years. Long after I had given up any thought of being a parent of small children, I was abruptly thrust back into the situation. Jenny was suddenly abandoned by her always unreliable husband, and left without any means of support. Since having her four daughters, she had not worked outside the home except for occasional temporary part-time jobs. She had devoted her time and energy to raising and caring for them. Now suddenly she had no economic support at all (or indeed any other kind of support). Kay and I did not hesitate to invite her to come to Coralville so that we could provide assistance until she got back on her feet.

Thus began my second career as a father of young children,

which lasted for eight years, until Jenny married a second time, this time to Steve, a man as good as Gregg was inadequate. Jenny soon got herself back on track, found a job and went back to school to prepare for a better job, while at the same time, dealing with a divorce and all that it entailed. To make this possible, Kay and I took most of the day-to-day parenting duties off her shoulders to leave her free to deal with the physical, economic, and emotional problems which a divorce usually brings.

These four girls were a delight to Kay and me. They brought much joy into our lives. BUT—like their mother, they had been going through turbulent times, and reacted like most children would react—they were somewhat wild and undisciplined, acting out their pain and bewilderment. It was imperative that some regularity and discipline must be imposed. My experience raising my own kids left me with one conviction—that I should never use any form of physical punishment on them. I concluded that I was smarter than that, and that I should be able to deal with the problems of four- to nine-year-old children without beating them.

One of my early chances to practice my new-found conviction was with Susy (six years old). Jenny had been running some errands in her car with the children along. At some point, she stopped to get a treat for them (perhaps a cookie). Susy had been misbehaving in the car and would not listen to Jenny, so she didn't give Susy one. Susy was truly incensed by the slight, and carried on even more as they headed back home. At one point she threw a full water bottle at Jenny, nearly causing her to swerve into another car. When they got home,

Jenny asked me to discipline Susy, thinking, I suspect, that I would spank her. Instead, I sat her down on the back steps and we talked—I don't know how long, perhaps as long as half an hour. I explained to her that what she had done was very dangerous, and described to her some of the possible consequences. She was very lucky, I said, that nothing bad had happened. We talked about why she had done it, and why her mother had disciplined her in the first place. By the end of this time, Susy was crying and promising never to do anything like that again. I believe that she even apologized to her mother. It was one of my early experiments in actually trying to reason with a misbehaving child, and I surprised myself at how effective it was.

Susy had a volatile temper as a child, and this certainly did not cure that. But it lighted the way for me to deal with the children in a new way, one I had never seriously tried before.

Two incidents related to Jessica (eight years old when they came to live with us) come to mind. Jessica was a very impetuous child. This was not all her fault, because she was afflicted with Attention Deficit and Hyperactivity Disorder (ADHD). She did take medication for it, but she hated the medication. She said she didn't like the way it made her feel. When she could get away with it, she didn't take it. The occasion which I relate was one of those times in which she did not take it. She and Anne (the oldest) were playing in the family/recreation room when they got into some argument, the substance of which is now lost in the mists of time. Jessica got so angry that, on impulse, she threw some foot powder into Anne's face (I have no idea what that was doing in the family room). This was a serious matter. It got into Anne's eyes and required a trip to the emergency room for treatment. When we got back from the hospital, Jessica was already trembling in fear of what would happen to her. I sat her down and we had a no nonsense talk about what she had done and the possible consequences. I admit I exaggerated the consequences, but I was still very angry. At the conclusion of this talk, l told Jessica that this kind of behavior required a very special kind of punishment, but I was not prepared to say at that time what it would be. I had to think it over, and would tell her tomorrow. Jessica spent a very worried twenty-four hours before I pronounced sentence on her. For the next week, I told her, she was to be her grandmother's shadow, and do whatever she could, or was told to do, to help her in all of her tasks. She was not to have any time to herself except what her grandmother specifically allowed her. Jessica was so relieved, that for a week she was a model helper, washing dishes, cleaning up, helping with the laundry, even cleaning out the refrigerator. All in all, it turned out to be quite a pleasure for both her and her grandmother. I don't think Jessica ever did figure out that the real punishment was not the week spent helping grandma, but the twenty-four hours she spent fearing what was going to happen to her.

The other incident I remember did not take place in my presence, but was told to me by Kay. Jessica had committed some act of defiance toward Kay and was definitely in need of correction. Kay told her that she was going to have to talk to me about her punishment. Jessica said to Kay, and I quote, "Can't you just spank me? If you tell Grandpa, he'll TALK to me."

When I heard that I knew I was on the right track.

XIX

SPELLING BEE

When I began to write this series of anecdotes, I thought of them as coming primarily from my own memories of growing up, and the trials and tribulations of trying to be an adult. I now find that my memories are also populated with many other people, many of them members of my many families (five, at last count)[7] with which we have shared our house, our home, and our lives. My grandchildren rampage through my memories with little regard for order, but with color, joy, and amazement (mine). So it is that I spend much of my time telling of their exploits and our interactions through the years.

This story features my oldest granddaughter, Anne. Although Anne has a wicked sense of humor and a lively sense of fun, you have to know her well to see that side of her. To the outside world, she appears as a serious, reserved, and dedicated scholar. As I write these words, she has recently become head of the Music Library and Professor of Music at Northern Colorado University, a goal which she has worked toward for many years.

This trait has manifested itself since childhood. Her mother Jenny tells of an incident which occurred when Anne was about six, when

---

[7]For those who aren't keeping count, they are:
Jenny and her four girls, 1994-2002
Beth and her three boys, 2004-2013
Laura, Al, and Morgan, 2014-2016
David, 2016-2019 (Can one person constitute a family?)
Morgan and James, 2020-2021

she was waiting with her mother in a doctor's office. Even at that age, she was like her grandfather in that she seldom could be found without a book. She was whiling away the time by reading what today would be called a chapter book. A woman seated next to her looked over at what she was reading, and declared, "My, that's a big book for such a little girl to be reading." Anne didn't say anything, but after a few moments, she closed her book and reached down to pick up another book, opened it up and began to study her Latin grammar!

When Anne was in seventh grade, she entered her school's spelling bee. She came in third, and was enthralled with it. She vowed that the next year she would win it. During the ensuing year, she studied words, pored over the dictionary, and bought an old beater of a typewriter so that she could type out lists of words as a means of memorizing them. In other words, she prepared as thoroughly as she could to accomplish her goal.

Came time for the spelling bee during her eighth-grade year and she was as thoroughly prepared for it as it was possible to be. And sure enough, she won. This was not the end of her ambition, however. Winning her school's contest meant that she could represent her school at the District Spelling Bee, which consisted of the schools in three or four counties. Came the evening of the district contest, and I drove her to Cedar Rapids for the bee. I confess that I was rather tense. I wanted her to do well, and it was pretty obvious that I was less certain than she was that she was prepared. As she sat there calmly spelling her way through word after word, I grew more and more tense. It was like watching the Chicago Cubs in the seventh game of the 2016 World Series, only much more personal. Finally there were three contestants left, and they were one by one given a word. The first two misspelled and were eliminated. Finally it was Anne's turn, and she was given her word. I don't remember what the word was, but it was all I could do to sit there and not spell it for her. I was totally tense, but she appeared and sounded totally calm as she spelled the word correctly and won the District Spelling Bee. I confess that I probably humiliated myself when I jumped up and threw my arms in the air. I was that happy and that proud of her.

Anne had now qualified for the State Spelling Bee, which was to be held at North High School in Des Moines. On the appointed day I drove her to Des Moines. The contest was to be held in a very large auditorium. There were more than fifty contestants from all over Iowa. When the spelldown began, it at once became apparent that not all of the contestants were equally prepared. Nerves and uncertainty were at once manifested in some of the contestants as they misspelled words that they might in other circumstances have spelled correctly. But after the first two or three rounds, these students were eliminated, and the real contest began. When Anne's turn came, she stood at the microphone as if there were ice water in her veins and spelled correctly word after word. Slowly the number of remaining contestants shrank, until there were approximately fifteen left. Then came Anne's turn again, and she confidently stepped to the microphone. I do not remember the word which she was given, but I subsequently learned that it was a technical geological term. I had never heard of the word, and one glance at Anne revealed that neither had she. She was visibly shaken by this unforeseen turn of events. As she struggled to decide how to spell it, I ran through several possibilities in my head and came up with the most likely (to my mind) spelling. After some hesitation she spelled it. I was wildly wrong, she was almost right. Almost, but not quite. She had one letter wrong—and thus ended her dream.

As she came back down the aisle to sit with me, I could see the tears running down her cheeks, and I realized for the first time that Anne not only *wanted* to win the contest, she *expected* to. This was a devastating defeat, and I wanted nothing so much as to put my arms around her and comfort her. As we sat there and watched as the spelling bee continued, I looked over at her. She was in such misery that I violated one of my cardinal rules, which I had tried to instill in the girls. Always, I told them, when you go to any public performance, especially amateur ones, whether it be a play or a concert, or any other, always stay till the end. It may not be very good, but you should stay out of courtesy to the performers. However good or bad, they are doing the best they can, and they deserve that courtesy. But looking over at her sitting there in such misery, I leaned over, and said, "Would you like to leave?" She just nodded, and so we did.

On the way home, we rode in silence for some time, but after a while we began to talk. I wanted her to know how proud of her I was, both for getting as far as she did in a truly difficult undertaking, and for doing it with such grace. "If I could," I said, "I would award you first prize. I can't do that, because first prize is a trip to the National Spelling Bee. But I can, and I will, award to you second prize."

Second prize was a *Webster's Unabridged Dictionary.* I thought she had earned, it, and I think it eased the sting of defeat, at least a little.

Next day Anne and I went down to the Barnes and Noble bookstore to buy the dictionary. I blithely assumed that the price would be under fifty dollars. Imagine my shock when I saw the price —$150. I swallowed, bit my tongue, and shelled out the whole amount. It was after all for my champion speller!

The last word (so to speak) on this matter came the next day when I read in the newspaper about the winner of the Spelling Bee. It seems the word which she correctly spelled to win the whole thing was a word which I had grilled Anne on the night before the contest!

XX

SNOW

I grew up in the Upper Midwest, and am consequently fully conversant with snow in its many facets. Snow can be by turns fun, beautiful, frightening, and magnificent. I have, in a long life. experienced snow in all of these facets. I sometimes wonder what it would have been like to have grown up and lived in a perpetually warm climate. I am sure it can have its compensations, but it seems that one is deprived if one does not have to deal with the difficulties of snow and cold and never has to consider the exigencies of weather when going about one's daily life. It seems too much like the life of the poor little rich boy who has everything given to him and never has to earn his own way.

Snow is FUN! Every child should have the chance to discover the joys of snow: making snowmen (or snowwomen!), building snow forts, snowball fights, and most of all, sledding! Sledding was one of the joys of my early childhood winter memories. In Bloomfield we lived about a block from a kind elderly couple named Ira and Hazel Wilkinson. They had no children of their own, but were kind to all the neighborhood kids—in particular, as I recall, to me. Their property included the most beautiful sledding hill that you could imagine, and all the neighborhood kids were welcome to join in the fun of sledding there when there was enough snow on the ground. I don't recall that we ever had adult supervision on that hill, but I am certain the Wilkinsons kept an eye on things. To my childhood eyes the hill was steep and long, and the exhilaration of gliding down on your sled at about 100 miles an hour was indescribable.[8] Our parents were quite tolerant of all this potential mayhem, but did have one inflexible rule. At the bottom of the hill was a street, and we were *never, ever* to slide into the street. That was tempting because on the other side of the street the slope continued down into "Toad Holler", a neglected mini—valley through which flowed a somnolent stream. It was the ambition of the older kids to try to slide all the way down to the bottom of Toad Holler and onto the ice of that stream. That was not an easy matter because the aforementioned street was "paved" with cinders. But on occasion we had ice storms, or a thaw and refreeze which coated the street with ice, and then the street was no barrier at all.

As a general rule, I obeyed, not because I was particularly obedient, but because I feared losing sledding privileges on this marvelous slope. On one occasion however (I must have been about seven), the conditions were perfect, and I couldn't resist. The ice just seemed to invite a long slide. The other kids were doing it, and probably egging me on, but I don't remember. I got on my sled at the top of the hill in the prone position, which for me was rather daring, and I took off. Down the hill, across the Wilkinson's driveway (usually the stopping place), into the fortunately empty street, across into Toad Holler, excited and happy. As I sailed along, however, I saw to my horror, that I was headed straight for a wooden fence, and I was

---

[8]As an adult, I once stopped in to visit the Wilkinsons, and was shocked to see how much that hill had shrunk. It was no longer than about fifty feet, and so gentle of slope that a speed of five mph would be scarcely attainable.

about to bash my brains in. I was too terrified to think that the obvious answer was to roll off my sled, so I kept going at flank speed. I did flatten myself the best I could on my sled and tucked my head down. Miraculously, I managed to slide under the fence (I am sure with about a micrometer of clearance) and kept on going down the hill. I do not remember exactly how far I got that day, but it is assuredly the farthest I ever attempted. Trudging back up the hill, I was so happy not to have bashed my brains in that I tamely stayed on the hill for the rest of the afternoon. Ah, sledding!!

Snow is BEAUTIFUL! When I was sixteen, we moved to Des Moines, where I had my senior year in high school. I met and was smitten by a young lady named Margaret Hellie. We went just about everywhere together, and I had many experiences which I might not otherwise have had were it not for her adventurous spirit. On Christmas Eve that year she invited me to go with her to the Christmas Eve service at the Plymouth Congregational Church, where she attended regularly. It was a nice service, and I enjoyed it in a kind of passive way. One of the features of the service was that the choir (quite a good one) opened the service by singing Benjamin Britten's "Ceremony of Carols". This was the first time I had heard this piece. My ear had not become attuned to the strange sounds and harmonies of this piece, and I was not sure whether I liked it or not. However I was intrigued enough that I wanted to hear it again, which I did the next two Christmas Eve services at Plymouth Congregational. The more times I attended the more entranced I was with the beauty of this service, and the "Ceremony of Carols" in particular.

The year following was a very busy one. I am not quite sure what the circumstances were, but for some reason, my aunt and uncle and two cousins were spending Christmas with us. My cousin Steve and I had been close since we were small children and spent time together every summer at our grandparents in Eddyville. Because of the crowded conditions, Steve and I were sharing a bed. We decided to go to bed rather early, so we hit the sack about 9:30 on Christmas Eve. We were both still too wired to go to sleep, and so we spent some time talking. It occurred to me that the Christmas Eve service would soon be starting at Plymouth Congregational, and I mentioned it to Steve. As I did so, I had a sudden desire to attend it again, and asked Steve is if he would like to go. He said yes, so we hurriedly dressed and left for the church. It was a clear and cold winter night. Everything seemed still, as if the world itself were holding its breath. The service was beautiful, and I was familiar enough with it that I could take it in almost in awe. The singing of the "Ceremony of Carols" in particular affected me. I had learned by then to love the piece, and do still to this day.

Following the service we walked outside into a much-altered world. During the service the skies had clouded up, and as we emerged, we walked into a picture postcard snowfall. Big white flakes were falling gently and glistening in the few lights which were on. It was a transfigured night. The snow was the benediction on the service itself. I have seldom felt, before or since, the sense of holiness and beauty that I felt that night. I do look for such occasions, and, rarely, I get a glimpse of them. I do not understand them, but I treasure them.

Yes, snow can be beautiful!

Snow is FRIGHTENING! Fun and beautiful, yes, but beware of its bite!

Kay and I met in the fall of 1957. We were soon spending most of our time, aside from classes, in each other's company. By Thanksgiving we were engaged, but few people knew it as yet. Christmas break was the first time we were going to be apart for any considerable time. She was returning to Columbia, Missouri to spend the holidays with her family, while I needed to stay in Des Moines because I had a job and other responsibilities. We agreed, however, that after New Year's I would come down to Columbia to meet her parents and bring her back to school.

My plan was to leave right after lunch to drive to Columbia. It was about a five-hour drive under normal circumstances, and I figured that would get me there not long after dark. My plans were disrupted, however, by my brother Bill, who thought he was being helpful. "You don't want to drive such a distance without a working radio. I can fix it for you in just a few minutes," he offered. I agreed that it would be very pleasant to have a working radio in my ten-year-old Chevy, so I agreed to wait.

Time passed as Bill worked on the radio. One hour. Two hours. I had waited long enough. "I'll drive without the radio." Bill is usually a mild-mannered agreeable person, but he has a stubborn streak. He wasn't about to quit in the middle of a job. There wasn't a lot I could do, since he had the guts of the dashboard spread out all over the front seat. So I sat and fumed while he tinkered away with what turned out to be a much more complicated job than he had originally thought. Finally about seven in the evening, he triumphantly announced that the radio was now working. It would help keep me awake, and thus I would have a safer journey. RIGHT!

As I left, the evening was a typical mid-winter Iowa evening. The temperature hovered around 10° and the air was crystalline. The sky was cloudless, and the stars shone with a special brightness. In other words it was a perfect evening for a drive. As I headed towards southern Iowa, however, this all changed. The sky began to cloud up, and the wind picked up. By the time I was just north of Ottumwa, a few flakes began to fill the air. By the time I got to Bloomfield, it was snowing hard, and snow was beginning to stick to the road. I was not a particularly experienced driver, but what experience I had was in Iowa, and I knew enough to slow down and pay close attention to what I was doing. South of Bloomfield and just north of the Missouri line are a series of roller-coaster hills, usually with deep ditches on either side of the highway in the valleys. By this time I was driving at about 45 mph and cussing at Bill because I knew this meant that I was going to be *really* late.

As I came up over the top of one of those hills and started down into the next valley, my car started to fishtail. I knew better than to try to put the brakes on, but I did try to slow down. It was no use, the car was not going to respond to anything I did. It was in full skid mode. As I came down the hill, I could feel the car fishtailing more widely with every swing. Finally I simply took my feet off of the pedals, grabbed the steering wheel with a death grip and hung on. There was nothing else I could do. I knew I was going to end up at the bottom of the ditch which along here was about twenty or more feet deep. As I reached the bottom of the hill the car did a 360° and came to rest exactly across both lanes of traffic. Luck had been with me in two respects. There had not yet been enough snow to cover up the gravel on the sides of the road. When my tires hit the gravel, it stopped all my sideways momentum. And there had been no one coming from the other direction. If there had been, there is no way that they could have stopped, or, under those circumstances, even slowed down. I would have been struck with considerable speed. Back in those days, before seatbelts, I would probably have been killed.

Now that I had been providentially spared, I returned my attention to my mission, but now my speed was 25 mph. I was going to be *really, really* late! But the farther I drove, the harder the snow fell, and now it was becoming, not a question of when I would arrive, but if! Highway 63 in northern Missouri is not exactly a main traffic artery, and I was practically the only driver out in this storm. No snowplows had ventured out and I was driving through heavier and heavier snow on the highway. Staying on the road was more instinct than sight. Then my windshield wiper started to freeze up, and I had to stop about every five miles to clear it off. I looked in vain for any all-night gas station or any place that might be open, but in vain. I dared not get off the highway to try to find a town. I did finally find one all night gas station/coffee shop, where I gratefully pulled in. The coffee was welcome, but the news was not. The report was that it was worse south of there. You must understand. I was twenty years old, and I knew that I was immortal, but even so, I began to get really scared. But there was nothing to do but plow ahead.

Finally when I reached Moberly, about thirty miles north of Columbia, the snow began to slack off, and I was able to make it through without further incident. It must have been about four in the morning when I pulled in, exhausted, and elated that I had made it through. Weather reports the next day reported that the area through which I had traveled had received about six inches of snow overnight.

I have lived all my life in the upper Midwest. I know that every winter there are a few people who get trapped in their cars during blizzards and do not survive. I never expected this to happen to me, but for a while I realized that it **was** a possibility. Make no mistake about it. That lovely, fun white stuff can be frightening, even deadly!

Snow is MAGNIFICENT! When you are out in a full-blown snowstorm it can be frightening. When you are in safe quarters and can observe a blizzard in safety, that same storm can be truly magnificent and awe-inspiring. I know that in the mountains of the west they sometimes measure snowfall in feet rather than in inches, but we flatlanders in the Midwest don't see storms like that—except in rare circumstances. A snowfall of six inches is a good hefty storm, one of twelve inches memorable. But what if we experienced one of those western storms in our flat lands where there are no mountains to break the force of the winds or at least confine it to mountain peaks and high valleys?

It happened in Illinois and Indiana in January of 1967. It was the most awe-inspiring snowstorm that I have ever experienced. We were living in Lakeville, Indiana at the time, a tiny town about ten miles south of South Bend. The weathermen had predicted a big storm, but nothing like this. Once the snow started, it would just not quit, and to make matters even more severe, there was a forty-mile-per-hour wind behind it. The snow fell for two days, perhaps longer. It was impossible to go anywhere, so everyone hunkered down and watched. Snow in that quantity together with wind of that velocity can do amazing things. By the time it was over, I had a snowdrift more than ten feet high directly outside my study window. We had received over two feet of snow from the storm, the most I have ever seen at one time. The town was completely transformed. Nothing moved. The highway through town was blocked, and it was several days before the snowplows could get it fully opened.

I revert back to the beginning of this essay. For our girls, this was big-time FUN. Beth was still a toddler, but Jenny and Laura loved it. They were scarcely taller than the snow was on the level, and the drifts must have seemed gigantic from their perspective. Heck, they seemed gigantic from my perspective! When Laura came in from playing in the snow, she was missing a boot. We didn't find it till spring.

For those of us living in a small town, it was an inconvenience, particularly for those who worked in South Bend, but all in all, it was one of those once-in-a-lifetime experiences which mostly provided stories to tell our grandchildren. But believe it or not, we were on the edges of this storm. Chicago was in the bullseye. They received perhaps twice as much snow as we did, about three and a half feet. It was probably the worst natural disaster ever to hit Chicago. What was mostly an inconvenience in a town of 900 was a calamity for a city of eight million—life-threatening to many, completely disrupting vital services for a long period of time. I believe that New York City experienced a storm like this back in the 1880s, in which hundreds of people died. Chicago was better organized and better prepared, but nevertheless the city was paralyzed for several days, and dozens of people died.

Magnificent is perhaps too tame a word for this event—perhaps the wrong word altogether. But that is how I remember it—a wondrous demonstration of Nature's power and our relative weakness in the face of it. As the effects of global warming become more apparent, we may have to face more events like this. What did they say in that old TV commercial? "It's not nice to mess with Mother Nature!" Ah, if we had only listened!

XXI

MOTHER

My mother was an aristocrat. There is no other way to describe the quiet pride with which she carried herself, nor the confidence with which she went through life. I do not mean that she was conceited or felt herself better than others. Rather, she knew her worth and the worth of the life she led and taught to her family. She came by this honestly. On her mother's side, her family, the Mulfords and Burrows, had been prominent for more than 350 years. Her distant ancestors had been among the first settlers and leaders of the community of Easthampton, Long Island, New York. 250 years ago, they had been early settlers and leaders of the English settlement in northeastern New Jersey, in what today is the city of Elizabeth. And 150 years ago, they were among the founders and leaders of Davenport, Iowa.

Her father's family, the Adamses? Not so much. They were commoners in the full sense of the word. The first Adams in this country, William, immigrated early in the nineteenth century from Scotland to New York. He was a common laborer who worked as a lumberjack in the primeval forests of the Catskill Mountains. Some of his sons were lumberjacks in later years in the old-growth forests of northern Pennsylvania. There appears to have been a spark of wanderlust in this family. One of my grandfather's uncles, James, in one of the few tracks he made in the historical record, was listed as "tramp" in the 1880 federal census. My grandfather, Carroll Adams, had a sister, Mary, who, according to Mother, was a wanderer all her life, drifting in and out of the family, showing up when she was destitute, and then disappearing for long stretches of time until she needed another assist.

My grandfather (whom I never knew) must, however, have had at least a spark of ambition in his soul, as well as the wanderlust that was endemic in the family. As a young man, he deserted the forests of Pennsylvania for the prairies of Iowa. There he found work as a laborer on my great-grandfather's farm on the outskirts of Davenport. Hired hand and boss's daughter were soon attracted to each other. There still exists a copy of what is probably the world's worst effort at love poetry, written by him when he was courting Ruth. In his youth he had been a schoolteacher, probably before he came to Iowa. In later years he owned and ran a truck farm near Davenport, and was one of the first rural mail carriers around the turn of the twentieth century. Who knows what he might have accomplished if he had not died of tuberculosis at the early age of forty-five?

My mother wasn't exactly strait-laced, but she knew right from wrong, and she wasn't taking any argument from anyone about that. I was told by my older brother Bob of one incident when he was a small boy. The family were traveling somewhere over a gravel country road. Farmers in that day were not always punctilious about keeping their livestock penned, and even when they did, the critters sometimes managed to stray. In this instance, a chicken ran out directly in front of the car, and Dad could not avoid hitting and killing it. There was no farmhouse nearby, so it wasn't possible to determine to whom the chicken belonged. Being practical people, mother and dad thought it would be a waste not to put the chicken to good use, since it was of no use to anybody else at this point. So they put it in the car, intending to have it for supper. After continuing on their way, however, and discussing the matter for several miles, they came to the conclusion that this might look to their young and impressionable children like stealing. So they stopped, replaced the chicken on the side of the road, and continued on their way. This occasion had a profound impact on my brother, and he remembered it with admiration for the rest of his life.

Another occasion concerned my younger brother Bill and my older brother Lew. Bill had serious medical problems after he was born. He was allergic to milk, and had to be fed for some time with a stomach tube. Mother learned how to do this unpleasant task with her usual acceptance of necessity, but she needed assistance to hold Bill while she inserted the tube, a procedure that any infant would likely object to. On this particular occasion, she had no one to help her but fourteen-year-old Lew, so he was drafted. This was a new, and obviously unpleasant task for him. As mom was inserting the tube she looked up at Lew, and saw that he was turning white, and showing signs of fainting. Without any hesitation, she reached up and slapped him across the cheek, saying, "Stay with me. I need your help. You can faint later."

She may not have been a superwoman, but I can honestly recall no instance in my childhood where she was unequal to any emergency.

Mother was the disciplinarian in the family. I never saw her lose her temper, although when faced with a disobedient child, she could appear pretty grim. Dad could administer punishment when called upon to do so. That usually involved a brief, and soon forgotten, spanking. Mother, however, was more subtle and more consistent. While she could certainly administer a spanking, she had more subtle ways of disciplining children. One summer evening when I was perhaps ten years old, I committed one of the unpardonable sins in the Hudson household. I was late for supper (usually the main family meal of the day when everyone was expected to sit down together). When I wandered in, everyone else was seated around the table eating. Mother didn't even look up from her meal. She simply said, "You're late. There's no supper for you. Go upstairs and get ready for bed." There was no appealing a sentence in our household, so I did as I was told. After about half an hour of lying in bed feeling sorry for myself, Mother came in with a tray of food. She didn't say anything, but simply set the tray where I could conveniently sit and eat. She turned around to leave, but at the door she turned and said, "I want you to know young man, that if it weren't for your father, you still wouldn't have any supper." That was one of the few times I ever saw my mother overruled by my dad, and to this day, I don't know quite why. I was guilty as sin.

I am grateful that, unlike in the case of my father, I was able to get to know my mother as an adult. Knowing her as one adult to another was a revelation. I do not recall that, after about age eighteen, she ever attempted to treat me as a child or pull rank. Whether she always approved of all I did or not (I am sure she did not), she treated me as an adult. I discovered that she had a marvelous sense of humor and had enthusiasms which could absorb her. We shared a good many interests, most especially genealogical and historical research. We had many an enjoyable and sometimes downright exciting times burrowing through dusty county records. We discovered the pleasure of prowling through strange cemeteries looking for ancestors and assorted relatives. We took trips together, most of which involved genealogical research, but were much more than just that. We visited historical and other sites. And sometimes, we just enjoyed sharing a dish of ice cream. In all of this we enjoyed one another's company. Mother or no, she was a delight to know.

One occasion I recall was when we were prowling through central Illinois looking for a cemetery in which we suspected that relatives were buried. After a lengthy search, we found it. It was located on top of a relatively high hill about a quarter of a mile from the road. To get to it we had to crawl through a barbed wire fence, clamber down a steep ravine, cross the stream at the bottom, clamber up the hill and over the locked gate into the cemetery. When I looked at the barriers, I told mother, "Why don't you wait here while I go up and check this out?" "Not on your life," she replied. "I'm coming with you." And she did. Not only did she face barbed wire, deep ravine, flowing stream, steep hill, and locked gate; she got there before I did! And she was 75!

She was a grand lady.

XXII

DAD

My father's family were mostly farmers and laborers. My grandfather, Frank Hudson, was sometimes listed as a plumber, which in those days often meant roof drainage and the installing of eaves and drainpipes. In my personal experience, he worked mostly as a roofer. He also worked for a time as a sawmill operator. I believe he mostly put his hand to whatever job was available to him. Like my other grandfather, he married the daughter of a well-to-do farmer, my grandmother, Nora Bell Linderman.

My grandmother had been married once before. There is a story behind this. She married when she was only sixteen, I would guess against her father's wishes (her mother had died when she was very young). The man she married turned out to be a brute. He beat her unmercifully. After about six months of the marriage, her sister dropped in to visit her one day and found her crying and covered with bruises. Her sister immediately took over. "This is enough," she is reported to have said, and forthwith took her back to her father's home. The ultimate result of her sister's intervention was a divorce. Several years later she married my grandfather.[9] My father was their oldest child.

Dad was a very positive character. He may not always have been right, but he was *never* wrong. The story is told of how, when he was

---

[9]A factor in her decision to marry Frank was undoubtedly the fact that his much older sister, Rose, was Nora's stepmother. She would have known him most or all of her life, and she knew what kind of man he was.

sixteen years old, he went to work for a grocer. The grocer had just purchased his first car, a Model T Ford. He was extremely proud of the car, especially as it was one of the first in Eddyville, Iowa. One day the grocer had some deliveries to make, but he didn't have the time to make them himself. He asked dad whether he knew how to drive. My father confidently said yes, although he had never driven a car in his life. The grocer believed him and gave him the car to make the deliveries. My father promptly wrecked the car. I never heard the aftermath of this tale, but it must have been entertaining, to say the least.

After he graduated from high school, dad enrolled in a Minneapolis Bible College, a decidedly fundamentalist school, which apparently appealed to him at the time. There still exists a letter which he wrote to his parents when he was there, in which he bragged about how orthodox he was, and how he was able to confound a minister who had modernist views. This may, however, have been a case of protesting too much, since after one year in the fundamentalist school, he enrolled in the Drake University Bible College, a much more progressive school. In his ministry he was religiously conservative, but he was certainly no fundamentalist. He embraced the Biblical scholarship which was taking place among the dominant Christian denominations of the day, and he read with appreciation the writings of theologians such as Reinhold and Richard Niebuhr. I remember his telling of arguments he had with fundamentalists, and how he was as certain that he was right as when, as a college freshmen, he had written his defense of fundamentalism.

However conservative he may have been theologically, He was socially progressive. In one of his first churches in Texas, he was asked shortly after he arrived to speak to the students at the Negro school (Texas schools were of course completely segregated in the 1920s). He was given instructions of how to find the school, but when the time came for him to speak, he could not find it. He sought out one of the elders of his church to try to find the right directions. He explained that when he had followed the directions he had been given, all he could find was a tumbledown shack. The elder replied "Yep. That's the school." My father did not say anything at the time, but the next Sunday, his sermon was a scathing condemnation of any community that would allow such a condition to exist. Children were children, black or white, and deserved the best that any community had to offer.[10]

There is an aftermath to the story. Several years later, after dad had left this church, he came back for a visit. The same elder whom he had consulted met him and said, "Come. There is something I want to show you." He took dad to the site of the Negro school, and lo and behold, there stood a sturdy and neat concrete block school in the place of the old shack. From our perspective that may not have been an adequate response, but for the time it represented the awakening of a community conscience for which my father was at least partially responsible.

---

[10]I heard this story from George Cherryhomes, who was a fourteen-year-old boy in the congregation that Sunday. He described how dad's eyes flashed as he delivered that sermon. It obviously made a deep impression on him. George, partly inspired by dad, later became a Disciples missionary and minister.

My father was a deeply proud man and he cared deeply for his family. He was also a practical man, and knew that some of things which his church frowned on were trivial and of little importance. Early in his ministry, soon after he had begun his service in one of his Texas churches, in an attempt to become better acquainted with merchants in the downtown area, he sauntered through the shopping district, stopping in the shops to introduce himself to them. In his walk down Main Street, he noticed some men playing checkers out on the sidewalk. Dad was a champion checkers player, and he stopped to watch for a while. After observing for a few minutes, he concluded that he could beat either of the men who were playing, and at the end of their game, he volunteered to take them on. They agreed, and dad defeated them both. He thought no more about it, but a few days later, an elder from his church called on him and said, "I hear that you have been seen playing checkers in public. You may not know it, but that is a gambling game in Texas, and it will do your reputation no good to be observed playing." Dad never again played checkers in public, but that did not mean that he stopped playing checkers in private. As far as he was concerned, it was a minor matter, and not worth making an issue about. Dad knew which things were important and which were not, and he would not let minor matters get in the way of the important ones.

Because of his sensitivity to public reputation, we PKs (preacher's kids) were expected to conform to the same standard. Card playing (with Playing Cards) was forbidden, because they were primarily known for and used in gambling. Dad did, however, love the card game of Rook, a game for which he had such a great love that it became something of an unofficial Hudson game, and continues so even to this day. In short, Dad loved games, but he would never do anything which he felt might imperil his important work as leader of the church and point man in the saving of souls. Although I never heard him put it that way, that is pretty much the way he saw it.

As I already have said, he was proud man, and he resented anyone who tried to diminish that pride. It was during the darkest depths of the Depression when he was serving his last church in Texas. There was little ready money available, and the church suffered right along with common people everywhere, who had little or no means of income. Giving to the church suffered greatly, and many weeks the church could not meet dad's salary. Dad resorted to the only means he had of feeding his growing family, which now consisted of four young children. He bought much of what he needed on credit. After this had been going on for some time, one of the merchants complained to an elder of the congregation. "Did you know that your minister is not paying his bills?" was how it was reported. The elder, knowing the circumstances in which Dad and Mom were laboring, did what he thought was a generous act. He went from business to business asking merchants for contributions to help the minister pay his bills. When dad heard about this, he was furious. He told the board, "If you pay me what you owe me, I can pay my own bills!" He then proceeded to find an old, much used Franklin stove and some gas lanterns, which he installed in the parsonage. He then went to the electric company and said, "Turn off my electricity." He also went to his neighbor and offered him a deal. "If you will let us fasten a hose to your outdoor spigot, we will pay for anything on your water bill over and above the basic charge." He then went to the water utility office and told them to turn off his water. Once he had made himself self-sufficient in basic services, he went to the church board and resigned. As soon as it was practical, he packed up his family and headed back to Iowa, in the same abrupt way he had packed up and headed for Texas several years earlier, not knowing what lay ahead. They stayed for three months with my grandparents until Dad found a church to serve in North English.

Dad had a lively sense of humor. He loved telling and hearing humorous stories. He had a deep rumbling laugh, which he freely gave rein to. Mother used to say that she never had any problem keeping track of dad in a crowd. She just waited until someone told a joke, and she would always be able to hear and recognize his laugh.

Dad loved music, and sang in a deep melodic baritone. He loved to sing what we then called Negro spirituals and other folk songs from various sources. I think it is at least partly from him that I learned to love music, particularly classical. Dad's favorite piece of music was Dvorak's "New World Symphony", especially the second movement, the "Largo". Mother chose it to be played at his funeral.

In small town Iowa in the 1940s, there were few occasions to hear classical music. There were occasional concerts broadcast on the radio. Then there were the band concerts which were a feature of many small towns in the 1940s. They were held weekly each summer, usually in the city park. Such concerts however, particularly in wartime, were often very heavy with marches and other military type music, some of it very good, but usually played very badly. And finally, there was the church. I know not about other churches, but in Dad's church, a great deal of thought (by Dad, if no one else), was given to the quality of the hymns. I learned many of the "old" warhorses, but also some of the best of the truly old hymns that have endured through the ages and survived.

From all of this I developed a taste for music which was sometimes at odds with that of my siblings, particularly my sister's. Her delight was in the currently popular music, which I disdained. Oddly enough, as an adult, I learned to appreciate the very music which my sister loved and which I, as a child, would have none of.

Dad was intensely devoted to his church and the ministry, but he knew the importance of relaxation. He grew up on the banks of the Des Moines River and he early learned the joys of fishing. He was a lifelong passionate fisherman. Among the many things which he passed on to his children was his love of fishing, a love which has now been passed on, yea, unto the third and fourth generation, and shows few signs of abating. Vacations almost always involved fishing. In the early years, vacations often took place with my grandparents in Eddyville and fishing was always on the agenda. Later, after Dad became minister of the Bloomfield Church, they often took place in a small cabin on the banks of Lake Wapello, a lake only a few miles away. Later still, after our move to Boone, when my older brothers had left the nest, and only my sister Beth, my younger brother Bill and I remained at home, vacations became more ambitious: journeys to Lake Whipple in Minnesota, and later still, Fox Lake in Wisconsin. Indeed, in our family, "vacation" was just another word for fishing.

I regret that I was never able to know my father as an adult. He died when I was just sixteen, before I really could get to know him as one adult to another. In retrospect, I believe that he was a complex man. He was a devoted minister, and a hard worker in ways that I have never been. He believed passionately in what he was doing, and perhaps at times took himself too seriously. Yet he could laugh at himself (and certainly at the foibles of others). He was, to me, a wonderful father, but he could be at times somewhat distant and mysterious. I was, especially in my younger years, somewhat in awe of him. He was inflexible in how he conceived that life should be rightly lived, and this created tension and conflict with my older brothers Dick and Lew, and my sister Beth. Dick ultimately gained dad's approbation, but I am not sure about Lew or Beth. I have heard Lew speak many times in an ambivalent manner about their relationship. And yet, as Lew himself eventually came to realize, he was perhaps the most like our father of all of us. Bob was perhaps more conventional, or maybe he was just less confrontational than my other siblings. Bill and I were too young when he died to have had the opportunity to rebel. Whether we would have or not I do not know.

XXIII

PETS, OR WHO OWNS WHO, ANYHOW?

As I look back over a long life, I realize that for much of my life, I have lived without a pet in residence. Aside from the occasional stray cat who would wander in and stay for a month or two and then travel on, I can count five pets in my life, three dogs and two cats. There was the dog of my childhood, Spot the Un-Wonder Dog. Then, when our children were young, we had two cats, Ebenezer the Hulk and Jeremiah the Feisty, and a dog, Sarah the Hysterical. Each was acquired at a separate time and under quite different circumstances, but the three spent much of their lives together in our household. And then there was Wilbur, my friend, the dog of our retirement.

When I was about eight, my parents surprised me and my brother by presenting us with a dog. I am not sure why, because, as I recall, neither Bill nor I had been asking for one. I do not know whether my father ever had a dog when he was a boy, but I do know that my mother had one, about which she still talked occasionally. It may have been her idea that we needed to have the experience of a pet. Whatever, Spot arrived very unexpectedly, and Bill and I welcomed her. Spot was by appearance a Cocker Spaniel, but was half again as big as the typical Cocker. My father opined that she must have had a springer spaniel somewhere in her ancestry. She had large splotches of black on a basically white coat, and big floppy ears. Bill and I quickly agreed that her name should be "Spot". (I think Bill and I were still under the spell of the Dick and Jane readers.)

Keeping dogs under restraint at all times was not a requirement in those days. Theoretically Spot was supposed to be attached to a leash which ran on the clothesline, except when she was running and playing with one of us. But she was adept at slipping her harness, and cruising our neighborhood in Boone. She made friends with a neighborhood reprobate Collie, who supposedly belonged to a family up the street. They, however, let him run free and, I suspect, only minimally took care of him. Despite our best efforts at controlling Spot, the two became notorious in the neighborhood. I don't recall all of their misdeeds, but I recall garbage cans raided, items stolen from neighbors' yards, and other mischief which caused no little stress among our neighbors. One time Spot brought home from her travels a saucepan of heavy aluminum with an attractive wooden handle. Despite mother's best efforts she never learned who this belonged to, so, being a practical woman, she decided she might as well use it. We still have that saucepan to this day, and use it occasionally. Thank you, Spot.

Fuzzie (the Collie) was definitely the leader in these forays, and Spot's mentor. One of our neighbors told us of a story about the neighborhood's most accomplished thief. It seems this neighbor had been having a disagreement with the milkman. On each delivery he was supposed to get two quarts of milk, but he began receiving only one. When he complained to the milkman, the milkman insisted that he had indeed been delivering two quarts. This went on for a while until one day when he went out early to get his milk, he discovered Fuzzie across the street in the park, busily prying off the top of a bottle of milk and lapping it up as it spilled out.

Spot was an apt student of our neighborhood's own Fagan, and we had our share of apologies and restorations to make. Our many efforts to restrain Spot were only minimally effective. The only effective solution would have been to make her a house dog, and mother emphatically vetoed this idea. After living for the last sixteen years with a house dog, I now understand why.

Spot was not the sharpest tool in the box. One example will suffice to explain what I mean. One day, we heard her whining and squealing, in a most unusual way. Her sounds were coming from the back porch, so we went to see what was the matter. There we found Spot sitting on a tack, in great distress but with not enough wit to get up off the offending point.

Despite her spending most of her time on the far side of the law, Spot was a sweet companion on many long hikes in the country, in romps in the park, and in general companionship. A boy could do worse than have a dog like Spot, the Un-Wonder Dog.

The next pet with which I had a serious relationship was a cat, Ebenezer the Hulk. It was, I think, Jenny's eighth Christmas when Kay and I decided that a good present for her would be a kitten. I went to the animal shelter to select one for her, or so I thought. My choice was a sweet-looking and quite docile white long-haired kitten. But while I was there, I noticed this yellow tiger kitten, who was making a big fuss. He climbed up the side of the cage and yowled pitifully. He was clearly saying "Take me. Please take me!" I could not resist. This kitten clearly needed a home, and needed one fast. So of course I succumbed. Instead of choosing a kitten, I was chosen.

When I took Ebenezer (he was named after my great-great grandfather) home and handed her to Kay the first thing this little ingrate did was to bite her on the neck. Woops! Anyway we had an animal with personality—and how! Jenny was, of course, delighted with her Christmas present. But we quickly learned the lesson every parent learns who presents a pet to a child. Guess who has to take care of it? This was not too much of a problem when we lived in Rockford. We lived on the edge of town and there was a lot of territory in which Ebenezer could roam. If he brought home the occasional mouse, it was no big deal. But when he brought home a baby kildeer, one of the charming birds which we enjoyed watching in the meadow adjacent to our house, the girls were upset. And I confess that I was not happy about it either.

Oh, and that cute kitten I brought home from the animal shelter? He quickly grew into a monster. At full growth he measured 36 inches from nose to the tip of his tail. He weighed perhaps twenty pounds, and he wasn't even overweight! There is a reason I call him The Hulk.

After he spent a couple of years as a free-roaming outdoor cat, we moved to Chicago, where Ebenezer had to adjust to being an apartment cat. I am not sure he ever got over the shock. But he survived, and in some senses thrived. When, a couple of years later, we moved again, this time to Coralville, laws there governing free-roaming pets being what they were (and are), he of necessity remained a house cat.

The next arrival in our menagerie was Jeremiah the Feisty.

Jeremiah was a stray kitten whose arrival in our household was strange, almost weird. As I recall, Jenny was at church camp, and we took this opportunity to take Laura and Beth to Stratford to spend a few days with their cousins there. After visiting with my brother Bob and his wife Dorothy for some time, Kay and I got in our car to return home to a whole week of kidlessness—a rare condition which we looked forward to. As we were about to drive off, Laura and Beth and a whole passel of cousins ran up to the car, carrying a cute little gray tiger kitten. "Can we keep her?" L and B cried, almost in unison. "Absolutely not." I said firmly. "One cat is enough." Despite some pleading, I was adamant. Disappointed, they went off with the kitten and their cousins. Thinking no more about it, we drove some 150 miles home.

When we got home, I got out of the car and the first thing I saw was a cute gray tiger kitten sitting on our back step. "How the heck did those kids slip that cat into our car?" was my first thought, followed immediately with the realization that they couldn't have, and in any case, wouldn't have. As soon as Kay saw it, she went into mother-mode. "It looks hungry. I'll get it some milk," was her first reaction. At that moment we were hooked. We were immediately the owners of another cat. Jeremiah (named for another ancestor) turned out to be a good addition to our menagerie (three kids, two cats), but to this day I swear those two kittens were enough alike to be twins.

Being a stray cat meant that Jeremiah had a few health problems that needed to be taken care of (ear mites, etc.), so he spent a few days at the vet until he was healthy enough to bring home. One of our concerns was how Ebenezer would respond to competition. Jeremiah was a smallish cat. At his fullest growth, he was never more than about seven or eight pounds to Ebenezer's twenty, and at this point he was still a half-grown kitten. Ebenezer's hunting instincts had been honed when we lived in Rockford, and we were afraid that he might see Jeremiah as prey. So we devised a plan whereby we could supervise their introduction and intervene if it got too rough. First, we put Jerry in our screened-in patio. and then we brought Ebenezer out, while we closely observed. The results were as surprising, I might say ludicrous, as I have ever seen. As soon as Ebenezer saw Jerry, he, as I had feared he would, dropped into his hunter's crouch and began to stalk. Jerry looked up, and saw this huge cat stalking him. First, he yawned, then he casually walked up to Ebenezer and swatted him on the nose. Right there he became Jerry the Feisty. Ebenezer was of course, taken aback. But it was the beginning of a beautiful friendship. They bonded almost immediately. Their favorite game was chase and catch. At any time, you might see Jerry being chased through the house by the Hulk. Ebenezer would catch him and sit on him, to the point where all you could see was a wagging tail, but let Jerry utter one small mew, and Ebenezer would immediately get up. It was great fun for both of them, and they never stopped playing chase-capture-release.

The third addition to our menagerie was Sarah the Hysterical. Our next-door neighbors owned two dogs, one of which was Sarah. Beth was a gregarious child and made friends with almost every adult she met. She was particularly friendly with our neighbors because of their two dogs, which she adored. When our neighbors moved, they said that they could only take one dog to their new home, and asked Beth if she would like to make a home for the other one. With Beth, there was never any question. Her only problem was overcoming my resistance. My answer was of course NO. We had all the pets we could handle. It took her a few days, but of course she won this unequal battle, and Sarah joined our happy little family—three daughters, two cats and a dog.

Sarah was a purebred Welsh Terrier, and if you are at all familiar with the breed, you know that they tend to be excitable. Sarah was way past excitable. She was somewhat on the far side of hysterical. Any little thing would send her into a fit of barking. I cannot say that we had a peaceful household before Sarah arrived, but now we were living in a constant state of agitation. Any little unexpected noise would set her off. The cats of course had the run of the house including the kitchen, and were not above jumping onto the counters to see what they could scrounge. We knew this and consequently kept all food locked up in various places and never left anything out. Sarah, however, felt that this was inappropriate behavior for the cats and appointed herself as kitchen warden. Anytime one of the cats got onto the counter, she went into a torrent of yipping. "Get off! Get off! Someone come quick and see what this awful cat is doing!" The cats, of course, ignored her.

The part of this behavior which most irritated Kay and me, was when she heard the milkman arrive with his delivery at about four in the morning. Sarah had to let everyone in the household know, racing from room to room, yapping and alerting us to imminent danger. The milkman was sometimes heard muttering, "Son of a bitch dog," and Kay, in her half-awake state, would say, "No. You've got that backward."

Our cats were reasonably healthy, but Sarah was another matter. She was allergic to everything, including herself. Seriously, she was allergic to her own fur, and we had to constantly give her medicine for this allergy. In the long run, this was her undoing, for the medicine eventually caused her to develop cancer, and we had, reluctantly, to say goodbye to her. For a few weeks after that sad event, the house seemed unnaturally quiet. She was a lunatic, but we loved her.

That leaves Wilbur, my friend, the dog of our retirement. But he deserves his own chapter, which may appear eventually.

XXIV

WHAT HAVE YOU READ? AND DOES IT MAKE ANY DIFFERENCE?

Over a long lifetime, I have read many books, some good, some bad, some important, some trivial, and probably far too many simply for entertainment, books without redeeming social value. I got to wondering recently, what books have I read which had a positive (or negative?) effect in the shaping of who I am today. Some sage once said that you are what you read, and there is probably a great deal of truth in that. When I look at a list of books that a Thomas Jefferson or a Felix Mendelssohn or any number of great men and women have read, I confess that I have spent a great deal of time entertaining myself, time which I could have spent educating myself and perhaps making myself more useful to others, or even to myself. Well, at my age, it is a little too late to mend my ways. I am who I am, and a large part of who I am has been molded by what I have read. So what have I read that has helped to form this very imperfect person?

Perhaps the earliest book I remember reading was Dr. Suess's very first book, *And To Think That I Saw It on Mulberry Street.* The characteristic silliness of the book is probably what captured my imagination, and I remember that I read it many times over.

By the time I was seven, I had graduated to story books, most notably the Dr. Doolittle books of Hugh Lofting. The appeal of animals who could not only speak, each in his own language, but who each had a wisdom to teach Dr. Doolittle, was fascinating. That a whole bunch of them together could have such interesting adventures, captured my imagination.[11] As a mature adult, I recognize now that there were some very bad racial stereotypes conveyed in these stories, but at the time I read them that went right over my head. Being raised in a progressive family where these attitudes were most definitely **not** taught, no doubt neutralized any negative effects that they might otherwise have had.

Being a somewhat lonely child, one who did not make friends easily, I found my adventures in books. I became a real library "mole", burrowing into the collections of the local public libraries in the towns where we lived. I remember for a while I was fascinated with the idea of wilderness. Books of life in the Rocky Mountains were a staple for a while, but the best of the books I read at that time had to be Jack London's *Call of the Wild.* In many ways I have never outgrown this fascination with the wilderness and wilderness living. I love the North Woods, where I have spent many vacations, and I regret that one of the great desires of my life will never be realized, a chance to visit, and perhaps even to live in Alaska.

From there I proceeded to some of the famous books about individuals or small groups of people who were by misfortune thrust on their own resources for their existence. Defoe's *Robinson Crusoe* was one such, but my two favorites were Johannes Wyss's *Swiss Family Robinson,* and most of all Jules Verne's *The Mysterious Island.* As an adult I realize that the islands on which the protagonists were

---

[11]I suppose that in serious literary studies these could be called hero journeys. To me they were just adventure.

marooned never existed, and could not exist. The geology, climatology, and most of all the biology of these places was impossible. But as a child in my pre-adolescent years, this didn't bother me at all. It was the adventure that counted.

Related to these books, but written more recently and hence more realistic in their settings are the "end of the world" books, in which a small group of people survive the disaster that depopulates the earth, by disease, or atomic warfare, or the invasion of aliens. I first encountered this type of book when I was about fourteen and I ran across a book called *Day of the Triffids*. It told of the invasion of a mobile, deadly, and semi-intelligent plant. I then discovered the marvelous *A Canticle for Liebowitz*, a novel of the aftermath (approximately 200 years later) of the effects of atomic warfare. But the best of them all in my estimation is the novel *Earth Abides*, which follows a small colony of humans who survived the devastation of a disease which wiped out 99% of the population of the world. This book has added interest in that it attempted to describe with some accuracy the effects on the world of the removal of the dominant species (humans) from the equation. These books and others like them I devoured as I discovered them in my teens and twenties.

I must also mention here one other amazing book which I discovered only a few years ago. It is *The World Without Us*, by Alan Weisman. It describes what would happen to the globe in our absence, if the entire human race were suddenly to disappear. It looks not only at what would happen to the works of humankind, skyscrapers, dams, and all the marvelous engineering products of the age, but the effects on the fauna and flora which have been dramatically affected for good or ill by the intentional and unintentional meddling of people. Truly, this book is a tour de force, and one of the most intriguing books I have read in a very long time.

There is another book of a very different sort that captured my childhood attention. My parents did not own a typical encyclopedia. Those multi-volume sets were far outside the price range of what my parents could afford. But we did own a book called the *Volume Encyclopedia.* It was a single volume containing about 3000 (!!!) pages. It was printed on super-thin, almost tissue-paper thin, paper, but nevertheless it was a massive book, at least six inches thick. We had this encyclopedia because, in order to put himself through college, my oldest brother Dick worked as a door-to-door book salesman, selling *Volume Encyclopedias.* My parents bought one to assist him. I am sure that the cost of even this one volume was far outside of their budget, but parents do what they can to encourage their children in laudable efforts.

This book was a godsend to me. From the age of seven or eight until well into my teen years, I constantly browsed in it, or used it as my reference book to answer specific questions or to give context and background to any subject in which I was currently interested. I remember especially reading and rereading the section on astronomy (I skipped the hard parts with the math). This was one of my passions when I was young, and I would sprawl out on the floor (the book was too heavy to hold on one's lap, and I was never one to sit at the table to read a book) and learn about the planets and the various kinds of stars, and be dazzled by the vast size of the universe. How much the interest in this book stimulated my interest in learning, and how much my interest in learning stimulated the use of this book I could not say. The book and my curiosity seemed simply to augment one another.

In my teen years, I was drawn to science fiction. For a time I wanted to read nothing else. There was some anxiety that accompanied this interest, because my father scorned what he called "pseudo-science". He tried to discourage me from reading "such trash", but it didn't work. It only made me feel guilty about reading it, as if it were a kind of esoteric pornography. My early interest in this genre was undoubtedly strong in the "space opera" type of story. But oddly enough, my interest in anything which could be labeled science fiction led me to read my first "serious" novel, *1984*, by George Orwell. I read this all unknowing that this was "serious" literature. What I remember most of all about this book is that I was almost physically sick after I finished the book. Nothing I had ever read to that point had had such a ghastly ending as did this book. The image of the protagonist running down the street yelling," I love Big Brother!" has stayed with me all these years. Even today it is to me a symbol of total defeat and degradation.[12] Reading Aldous Huxley's *Brave New World* had a similar, if less intense, impact.

---

[12]This episode in my life reminds me of my daughter Jenny, who when she was about ten years old decided to read William Shirer's *Rise and Fall of the Third Reich*. What she tackled was a revised and much shortened version of Shirer's original huge tome, but still very graphic. One day as I was taking her to school, she said she felt sick, and asked me to take her back home. I learned later that she had been reading this book in the back seat, and the account of German atrocities had caused her to become physically ill. Like father, like daughter!

My college years were years of discovery. I was a religion major (later religion and philosophy). When I look back on it, when I entered Drake as a freshman, I was incredibly arrogant. I was convinced that I could read and understand any book if I put my mind to it. This arrogance did not last long. The first semester I took an introductory class in religion under Dr. Dale Miller. He assigned each of us in the class to read a book on theology and to write a report on it. The book he assigned me was a book by a famous theologian, Daniel Day Williams, *God's Grace and Man's Hope.* I confidently began to read it—and got about ten pages in. I remember sitting on the steps of University Christian Church, across the street from the University and reading the same page over and over again. I had no idea what it was about. It was a humbling experience. I finally went to Dr. Miller and told him about the trouble I was having. "I understand almost all the words in the book, but they're put together in ways that have me totally confused," I explained. He laughed and said that was a common experience when first reading theology. He confessed that he had had a similar experience. "Moreover," he said, "you won't understand the second book of theology you read, nor the third. Along about the fourth book you'll begin to get an idea what it's about."

He was almost right. But there are some books by highly respected theologians that to this day I cannot read with any degree of comprehension. Such a book is Paul Tillich's *Systematic Theology* that I tried to read in seminary. I got about fifty pages in, and gave up in total confusion. I kept this three-volume set in the hope that someday I would be able to read it with some degree of comprehension. A few years ago I got it out and decided to give it another try. This time I got about one hundred pages read, and then gave up in despair. This work, and some others, keep me humble about my intellectual capabilities, and that's probably a good thing.

This sounds as if the books which influenced me professionally the most are the ones that I couldn't (and still can't) understand. That is at least partly right; if I had truly been able to grasp these esoteric works, I might today be a theology professor teaching at some obscure denominational college in North Nowhere, Montana (or at least retired from there). But that is only partly true. There are many works which I read with appreciation and at least partly with understanding. Some of those works have helped my understanding of life and of our place in the universe. Reinhold Niebuhr's *Moral Man and Immoral Society* made a powerful argument for what he called "Christian realism," and has helped me to shape my understanding of the Christian religion in its interaction with modern society.

Richard Niebuhr was the brother of Reinhold. His book, *The Meaning of Revelation* is perhaps the single most important book I have ever read. It has shaped my theology and my understanding of life. His attempt to reconcile the partial and conditional nature of all of human experience with the revelation of an eternal and unchanging God was, and is, compelling to me. The simple answer which he offered is, "You can't," but that a partial and socially conditioned revelation is not thereby invalid, any more than the laws of physics are invalid because they too are conditioned by our social experience. I have gone back and reread this book several times, which is something I almost never do. I still find new wisdom in this book, socially conditioned as it is, along with all other human thought.

So what reading has formed my transition from would-be theologian to historian? I admit to being a romantic historian, one who finds joy in reading and studying the field, especially of American history, for the sheer pleasure of it. Some of it can be enlightening, as is the book I am currently reading, *These Truths: A History of the United States*, by Jill Lepore, which is a history of the struggle between exclusion and inclusion in American society from the earliest times to the present. Such books shed considerable light and perspective on the somewhat alarming times in which we are currently living. Others are more simply entertaining, as is the novel, *House Divided*, by Ben Ames Williams, a book I read many years ago, a novel about the southern relatives of Abraham Lincoln during the Civil War. That book probably sparked my interest in the Civil War, an interest which continues to this day.

I must stop this. As I ponder, more and more books come to mind, and if I let myself, I will maunder on endlessly, like the old man I am. Suffice it to say that reading to me has for my entire life, been both pleasure and education. Both continue unabated in this, my eighty-third year, and I trust this will continue so long as I do. Happy reading!

XXV

EULOGY FOR KAY

This eulogy was presented by our pastor, Jill Cameron Michel at the memorial service for Kay on September 1, 2020. I will be eternally grateful to Jill for being able to express Kay's life so well and with such understanding.

—David

There are many things that feel different right now than what we expected. Not only do we tend to live with this naivete that the people we love will live forever, but when death occurs we have certain rituals that generally take place—rituals that tend to involve lots of people, lots of handshakes and hugs, lots of food. So, right now, the fact that we are living in the midst of a pandemic, means that we are currently unable to gather in the ways to which we have grown accustomed.

And yet, still we gather. We gather in smaller groups. We gather with masks and physical distancing. We gather via the Internet. But we find ways to gather because when a life matters, we must celebrate. And so, here we are today—some in person, some virtually—but all gathered to claim again that life matters and that Kay's life mattered to us.

Vivian Kay Hudson was born February 24, 1937 in Vinton, Iowa. She was the fourth child born to Wilbur and Florence Williams. It is important to note that she was fourth because she did not arrive alone.

Rather, just an hour or so later, she was joined by her twin brother, Vince. But even though they shared 83 birthdays, it always mattered to Vivian Kay that she was the older of the two.

As you know well, Kay grew up in a family with faith and music as core values. Her father was a pastor so the church was central to their family life. But for Kay it wasn't just about his job or a place they went on Sundays. That foundation wasn't just about loyalty to an organization. Rather, she developed a deep faith that carried her through life and confidently into death.

As a musical family, performing started young. Little Vivian and Vince, just a few years old, were known to stand on the table and sing, "You Are My Sunshine." And music accompanied them through their childhood into adulthood where music and performance not only were part of who they were, but part of what they passed on to the next generation.

While there were many things from her family of origin that she held dear and carried with her into adulthood, the name Vivian was not one of them. Instead, when they moved to Columbia, Missouri where she would graduate from high school, she decided to use her middle name and started to be called Kay. So, for most of us, that is the name we knew her by.

It was Kay Williams, a transfer student from Christian College in Columbia, who David Hudson met the fall of his junior year at Drake. Both religion majors, both from Disciples churches, both pastors' kids (whose fathers, they would discover, knew each other), both people with solid midwestern values, they hit it off immediately. Dave figured she was smart, she was funny, (and let's be honest, she was pretty), and she liked him—so he'd better act. By the time Thanksgiving came that fall, they were engaged to be married. As soon as they graduated in the spring of 1959, they made it official.

David and Kay had the privilege of sharing over 61 years of marriage with each other. That marriage worked because of a combination of shared core values along with enough personality differences to keep things interesting. After all, Kay was intuitive, while David is logical. Kay was spontaneous, while David prefers a plan. Kay didn't mind things scattered about, while David values order. And yet, differences that can be (and some days were) challenging, allowed them to complement each other and to be more whole when they were together.

It wasn't long after marrying that Dave and Kay expanded their family. Three daughters—Jenny, Laura, and Beth—were added. Kay treasured her role as a mother. She sang you all to sleep at night and instilled in you a love of music. She modeled for you that women could be many things as she both raised a family and worked outside the home. She taught you that it was good to try new things and to challenge yourself—something she exhibited when she took on a job teaching a third grade class that had been through four teachers in less than two months, and something she modeled again when she returned to school, as middle aged person, to pursue her PhD in English Literature with a specialty in Medieval Studies. And even though she did not use that degree professionally, she never regretted it. After all, she learned and grew through the process and she achieved something many won't even try.

Kay cannot be represented in one word or idea... she was many-faceted.

She loved bright colors and perhaps, even more, she loved shopping for bright-colored clothes (she called this retail therapy), never missing an opportunity to dress for the season or holiday. Even as her eyesight failed, when she was shopping for clothes, she could always find a good deal!

Kay was fun and had a wicked sense of humor. Even in the midst of the challenges of aging, she often chose to laugh at what could otherwise be frustrating.

Kay had a sixth sense about things. Maybe she was even a little psychic. After all, there is more than one story of her knowing things she had no logical reason to know... like the details of that time David ran into an ex-girlfriend on the bus. When Kay, who had been out of town at the time, knew every detail down to which seat she had been sitting in, both she and Dave marveled at her ability.

Kay was comfortable in both traditional and non-traditional roles, pleased to be a wife and mother, but also discovering joy in her work and her studies. And as she grew into adulthood she embraced progressive ideas about the role of women and found security in expressing them.

Kay was a storyteller. She had a story for everything. And if you pointed out that you had heard the story before she would just invite you to sit back and prepare to hear it again.

Kay was a people person. This was evident whether she was

visiting with church friends before and after worship on Sunday mornings, or opening her home to you, her children and grandchildren. People mattered to Kay.

Kay was a musician, a gift she shared with her students, with the congregations she was part of, and in a special way with you, her children and grandchildren, many of you whom are musicians in your own right.

Kay was strong and determined, something in her later years she was willing to admit she got from her own mother. "Just keep going," was Kay's mantra, as it had been her mom's.

Kay didn't believe in being coy—rather her "yes" meant yes and her "no" meant no. She lived by the rule that if you are invited to do something and you can and want to say yes, then by all means, do. If not, just say no and don't worry about it.

Kay was a person of faith. You all know that well. Her faith was important to her. And she continued to grow in faith throughout her life. It was something about which she was willing to ask difficult questions, and of which she was willing to embrace the mystery.

Kay's favorite Bible story was the story that takes place on the Road to Emmaus. That story occurs after Jesus' death and resurrection. Two followers of Jesus are walking home, grieving, trying to comprehend what's been going on. A stranger joins them on the road and they talk after, and as evening comes, they invite him to stay with them and to share a meal. It is there at the table—in the breaking of bread—that they recognize the stranger as the resurrected Jesus. In that moment, even though they didn't know exactly how, they knew with confidence that the divine presence had been with them all along. The story culminates in a beautiful verse that says, "Were not our hearts burning within us while he was talking to us on the road…?" (Luke 24:32, NRSV).

I don't know exactly what it was in that passage that Kay loved, but I can imagine that she embraced both the mystery of it as well as the assurance that even when we don't recognize it to be true, God is with us. I also suspect she was drawn to the idea that even after death, life remains.

Today as we remember Kay and celebrate her life, we also celebrate her faith. For in these last years as her body has given her more challenges, and especially in these recent months as it seemed she had a sense that the end of her life was near, Kay was not deterred from her confidence that death was not an end but a new beginning. While we don't know exactly what happens when this life ends, Kay was confident that God would greet her, that she would be reunited with her parents, and that perhaps she would even get to meet the great musician, Felix Mendelssohn.

We have gathered to celebrate Kay. Here in this room you all represent those who knew her best. A brother who brought out the joy in her. A husband with whom she partnered, who she pushed and encouraged, who she walked beside and sometimes led. Children and grandchildren who always knew they were loved and who have lived with the confidence that Kay would always welcome you home and give you a safe place to land.

Today we claim that it is has been a gift to share this life with her… we claim that our lives are better for having known her… we claim that we know more of God's love because we were loved by Kay.

XXVI

AFTERNOON ON MY BACK PORCH

There is a stillness on my back porch, like the stillness of the deep
woods.

On a summer day when I sit there, there are many sounds, but they
don't break the stillness—

The distant traffic sounds from the interstate—the occasional
car that rolls down our street—the barking of our neighbor's dog—the
far—off buzz of a lawnmower —

All of these are sounds as if from another world, one that has
nothing to do with me.

Instead, I hear the controversy of birds—the chirring of locusts
—the occasional rustle of a passing squirrel. When a light breeze stirs
the leaves, it is like an ostinato that joins these sounds in a summer
symphony accompanying the stillness.

I could sit here forever, caught in this quiet harmony.
But then my dog wants to go in.

XXVII
VIGILANCE (WILBUR)

My dog enters the outer world like a Kentucky pioneer.

He pauses at the top of the stairs—

Sniffs the air and peers from side to side

Looking for Indian sign.

When satisfied there is none he descends,

still alert for any danger.

When he is in the yard, I think he imagines his remote ancestors,

alert for prey and ready to defend his territory.

No wolf or big cat or man dare challenge him

He is fierce and vigilant.

He owns this territory.

Even though he is only nine inches tall.